THE *Last* BREAKUP

To our beloved
Son. We love
you so much.
God bless you always
♥ Mom+Dad

THE *Last* BREAKUP

Finding new life and true love
just when all hope seemed lost

Mark Johnston with
Rebecca Johnston

TreasureLifeMedia.Com

The Last Breakup

© 2019 by Mark F Johnston

Editing, design, layout, and publishing: Mark F. Johnston
Biblical advisory and support: Daniel J. Lynch, Jacob Coleman

ISBN-13: 978-0-9663917-1-8

Printed in the United States of America.

To God the Father,
our Lord and Savior Jesus Christ,
and every grace-filled heart who told us the truth in
love and led us to the Light, just when all hope seemed
lost. To our beautiful and talented son and daughter, our
parents, dear friends, and family members. And in
loving memory of Fred, Sher, Aunt Millie, and Michael.
Thank you.
We
love
you.

"Sanctify them through thy truth; thy word is truth."
John 17:17

"Not to us, O Lord, not to us, but to *your* name we give glory, Because of Your mercy, Because of Your truth."
Psalms 115 © NKJV

Contents

Introduction

Dear friends old and new,

In 2007 when someone first suggested we write a book to tell our story, our first reaction was "Not a chance." We shuddered at the thought of sharing our dirty laundry, and we couldn't fathom how our story—the textbook poster child for what <u>not</u> to do in life and marriage—could be of any value to anyone.

But a few years later, after hearing so many people ask us to reveal the "secret" to our marriage and friendship, we came to realize we were miraculously no longer a cautionary tale of what *not* to do, but a powerful living testimony of what is possible with Grace and faith the size of a mustard seed.

One thing led to the next, and in the fall of 2017 we were moved to write the book. 22 months and 7,500 hours of writing and conferring later, by the grace of God and faith, here we are.

Some might wonder why we chose to include so many details such as: injuries and recoveries, conversations with friends, attempts to self-heal, arguments, epiphanies, etc. In other words: why not just share what we learned and skip the drama? In short, we feel called to witness, and we've come to believe our story, dirty laundry and all, is the most effective way to testify God's transformative power.

So, while our exact trials (such as our marriage woes, mental and emotional states, and so forth) might not be relatable to some people, we believe both the causes and outcomes of them are common (which is affirmed in 1 Corinthians 10:13), and therefore there is utility in sharing them.

We also want to encourage more people to witness for the glory of God and saving of souls. To be sure, the world is filled with countless resources that teach about God's power and tell us how to harness it; but in our view, there aren't enough personal testimonies that actually prove His power. That is, we have a surplus of teachers and preachers, and not enough actual witnesses.

So this is us, with our hearts on our sleeves, not teaching or preaching, but bearing witness to the truth and resurrection power of Jesus Christ. We hope our witness inspires people from all walks of life and belief systems to surrender and put all their Hope in our Creator, so they can come to know His love and find all the truth, belonging, worth, and sweet *peace* that we believe every soul is ultimately seeking.

We pray you suspend your preconceived notions before reading this and enter through the door with an open heart and mind. We pray our testimony is an abundant blessing of truth to you. And above all, we pray our testimony glorifies God the Father in heaven and His Son, Jesus Christ.

Mark and Rebecca
September 23, 2019

1: Shattered

"And if a house is divided against itself, that house cannot stand" -Mark 3:25 (NJKV)

Mark: *"WATCH OUT!!"* I screamed at the top of my lungs from inside the garage. It was a couple hours before the start of our divorce moving sale, and I was hoping to save a petite elderly woman from being slammed in the back of the head by a falling steel beam. The 8-foot beam was part of my disassembled squat rack (an exercise machine), and the woman had just tripped on it after slipping into the garage without my knowledge.

Thankfully, my primal shriek caused her to turn and look in the direction I was pointing *just* in the nick of time. By the grace of God, the beam missed her head by a hair and instead crashed to the floor—shattering an expensive crystal set with an ear-splitting *"CLANG-CRASHHH!!"*

With my heart still pounding like a jackhammer, I carefully tip-toed over the glistening crystal shards, moved the beam out of the way, and asked the trembling woman if she was alright. Nodding in the affirmative, she pulled her sock down to reveal a little red mark where the beam had grazed her foot. Fortunately, it was just a minor scratch. I was not a spiritual person, but I thanked God repeatedly.

"Ma'am I'm very sorry," I said gently, "but this is why I told you earlier we weren't ready to start the garage sale and asked you not to go in the garage."

It wasn't until she forced a smile and replied in a thick accent, "S'OK, S'OK," that I realized she probably didn't understand English. *Ugh. Just my luck.*

As she shuffled down the driveway to leave, I was about to wish her well when my mother-in-law (who had arrived just in time to witness the mishap), quipped, "Don't bother suing him, he and my daughter are divorcing, and she took aaaaall his money."

Though my soon-to-be-ex, Rebecca, hadn't actually taken all the money, the comic relief was welcome, and I couldn't help but exhale a nervous laugh. I felt a little better when the woman made a kicking motion with her leg and reassured me "S'OK," one more time before getting in her jam-packed minivan and speeding off.

As if on cue, Rebecca pulled up just in time to see me waving goodbye to the woman. Upon exiting her car, she inquired, "Who was that?" When I told her what happened she huffed, "Wow! Everything we do turns into a fiasco. I'll be sooo happy when I don't have to deal with *this* anymore."

By "this" she was referring to the 14-year crazy train voyage we loosely referred to as a marriage. She had already moved out of our "dream home" and clearly wasn't happy about returning to help me sell our stuff. Having witnessed enough drama for the day, I kept my distance and treaded lightly to avoid sparking another meltdown.

A Few Months Earlier (Some background)

Rebecca: A few months before the fiasco moving sale, after a decade and a half of what felt like aimless sailing on rough seas, our marriage ship ran aground and finally sank for good. What went wrong? Here's a brief account (with the aid of hindsight).

In a nutshell, we fell in love and took Christian wedding vows, but when the honeymoon wore off so did our desire to please each other. Consequently, our marriage gradually devolved from a "match made in heaven" to a war of stubborn wills.

Then came resentment, transgression, seeking fulfillment outside the marriage, heartbreak, distrust, hostility, scars that wouldn't heal, and ultimately irreconcilable differences that made it impossible to peacefully coexist.

It seemed to me, the only reason we stayed afloat so long was because every time we sprang another leak, Mark put on his "fix it" hat and convinced me we could patch it up. We tried counseling, going to church, self-help, new promises and more; but in the end they were only band-aids, and when they inevitably failed, we sank again... and again... and again.

Mark: If doing the same thing and expecting a different outcome is the definition of insane, then our marriage was definitely a circus of insanity.

Moreover, after *seven* breakups and makeups (yes, seven) it was an embarrassing soap opera. What we didn't realize was that every time we got back together and didn't resolve the root problem, more baggage piled on our backs, and eventually the load became too heavy to carry and crushed us.

It's not that we didn't search for root causes. We just couldn't agree on who owned them.

I blamed Rebecca. She wanted me to be her everything, and when I failed to live up to her idealistic "knight-in-shining-armor" expectations she became resentful, indifferent, and distant. Not only that, but she didn't support any of my aspirations, was hyper-emotional, and her flighty nature worried me non-stop. When it reached the point where she avoided being at home, I knew the end was near.

Rebecca: It's true that I avoided being home, but only because we had no "home." We had a house, a nice one in fact, but it wasn't a home because there was very little sense of family and very little to no love and belonging.

I blamed Mark. His heart was devoted to his job and many other pursuits, and marriage and family weren't high on his list. He was hyper-competitive and domineering, put all his focus and resources into his goals, and rarely spent quality time with me (unless it was something he enjoyed). Eventually I felt no more valuable than a housekeeper with benefits and finally got sick of being with someone who loved their ambitions more than me.

Mark: In my estimation at the time, I loved Rebecca and was endlessly frustrated that she couldn't see it. For me, *love* meant providing, protecting, and endurance—as in sticking it out for the sake of keeping promises. My parents had stuck it out for 40+ years, and I was determined to follow in their footsteps. Hence, I tried everything in my power to meet Rebecca's endless demands but could never make her happy—which was demoralizing, maddening, and exhausting.

Rebecca: Yes, Mark provided and looked out for us, but I believed there was much more to love and marriage than welfare. To me, "sticking it out" wasn't enough, especially if it meant being married to someone who treated marriage (and me) like it was a major burden and inconvenience that stood in the way of their dreams.

But it's important to reiterate we're speaking in hindsight. At the time this was happening we didn't communicate our beliefs and grievances so clearly to each other. Neither of us wanted to hear the other's feelings out of fear of a meltdown, so we hid them from each other and instead walked on eggshells. The truth was not welcome in our home.

Not that I even knew what my true feelings were. All I knew was that we had totally irreconcilable differences, Mark was never going to change and be the husband I wanted, I was numb and exhausted, and my only hope for peace and happiness after 14 years of mostly war was divorce.

Mark: I finally threw up my hands and agreed. When we informed friends and family we were *really* calling it quits ("for *real* this time!") they weren't shocked. With a front row seat to our rollercoaster relationship, most were actually relieved. In our recollection no one tried to persuade us to stay together. Then again, given how erratic our marriage was, who could blame them?

Rebecca: We filed a couple days after I moved out of our family home. The initial plan was for Mark to get a roommate and stay for a while so our kids could have some stability. But like everything else, that was a fiasco too, so we finally agreed to sell the house. And that brings us back to the fiasco moving sale—which started with the violent passing of my crystal set.

That's a Wrap

Mark: Once I finally cleaned up the garage after the squat rack fiasco, we kicked off the moving sale and proceeded to sell many things we acquired together. It was all quite sad, and my heart was heavy all day as Rebecca and I stayed on opposite ends of the driveway... and universe.

Rebecca: I felt very different. I was glad to see everything connected to our crazy train sell. When the moving sale was finally over, I celebrated as I drove away. As far as I knew, I was finally rolling down an awesome road to a whole new life. Though I was feeling a little unsettled about my future, I was elated to be free.

Mark: After the moving sale ended, I went inside, grabbed a cold beer, and plopped on the floor in an exhausted heap. Laying under the ceiling fan I remember thinking how similar the fan's circular motion was to our marriage... round and round and round. *If nothing else*, I reasoned, *it was a relief to finally leave the circus life and hopefully find some peace.*

But that didn't quell my resentment from having *wasted* 14 precious years of my life trying to revive a horse that probably died many years ago. I couldn't believe the time and money burned! The toil!

Like the shattered crystal in the garbage can outside, my life was now in pieces, and I had no idea how to rebuild it. Feeling cheated and exhausted, I flipped a beer bottle cap across the room at a stack of boxes and growled, "Thanks for nothing!"

Rebecca: I didn't feel bitter at all (initially). The only thing I was miffed about was that we lived in a state where couples are required to wait *six months* for their divorce to be official.

That meant we wouldn't be legally unhitched until the state approved our dissolution. And that meant there was plenty of time for Mark to attempt another "fix it" job to patch us up again. I vowed to stand firm and never allow him to change my mind or heart. *Never again!*

It would be the most unpredictable and astonishing six months of our lives.

The *Last* Breakup

2: Warrior Down

"My days have passed; my plans are shattered; along with my heart's desires." -Job 17:11 (ISV)

"The swift will not escape, the strong will not muster their strength, and the warrior will not save his life." -Amos 2:14 (NIV)

Mark: A few weeks down divorce road I was trying to pick up the shattered pieces of my life and rebuild. Having endured multiple separations I was sadly familiar with the pain cycle, but the official divorce filing added a tragic sense of permanent loss that I wasn't prepared for. On top of that, I was wracked with stress and worry because I had lost my job and, despite my best efforts, couldn't find a new one.

Nevertheless, I was a US Army-trained warrior and fierce competitor, and I hated—I mean *hated*—losing. I reasoned as long as I still had my health and could exercise and compete, I could get through anything, as always.

I vowed to myself: "I will rise again out of the ashes like a Phoenix. I will rebuild the best life ever for myself. I will improvise, adapt, and overcome! *Hoowa!*" Oh, how God must have been laughing at that moment.

Breakdown

Owing to a lifetime of "you-made-your-bed-now-man-up-and-lie-in-it" self-help conditioning, I internalized my aggressions and attempted to purge them via weightlifting and basketball, as always. Grunting and growling my angst away seemed to be going fine until...

Boom. One day in the garage while attempting to lift far too much weight on my squat rack (yes, the same one the lady tripped on at the moving sale) I suffered a devastating back injury. It happened when I squatted down and suddenly realized I didn't have enough strength to stand back up. In my haste to set up the equipment, I forgot to install the safety catches. Story of my life.

"Holy $#@%&!!" I grunted. I was frozen in the squat position with 300 pounds of steel on my back and no way to escape.

I panicked and tried to jerk upward as hard as I could. Bad idea. Suddenly I felt a searing pain in my lower back, my knees buckled, and I crashed to the floor with the barbell on top of me. *"UUUUUAAARCGH!"*

After carefully sliding out from under the weight, I crawled back into the house on all fours like a wounded animal and called Rebecca to break the news. "I threw my back out and can't move," I groaned.

"Not again!" she said incredulously.

"I can't take the kids."

"But I have plans!"

"Sorry!"

"Whatever," she huffed, "I will handle it, as always." Then the line went dead. I couldn't believe how insensitive she was.

Rebecca: I was insensitive because that wasn't the first time Mark's addiction to extreme exercise resulted in a debilitating injury. I was sick of his fiascos, and I was tired of being on the receiving end of his emergency calls.

Mark: The next morning the pain was so bad I couldn't get out of bed. Three weeks later it was even worse. People implored me to see a doctor, but my warrior pride wouldn't hear of it. I was inching along for a while until the pain spread to my legs and upper back. Fearing my spine was damaged severely, I finally caved and made a doctor's appointment.

After x-rays, an MRI, and an hour on a gurney waiting for the results, the doctor met with me in a small exam room. He got right down to business. "You have a sprained back and pretty severe disk injury. Your options are steroid shots, which aren't guaranteed to work, or surgery."

Oof. He might as well have said "poison or firing squad." No way was I going under the knife or needle. I told him I would take my chances the injury would heal on its own. He smiled cordially and said, "Ok, your call." But his eyes said something more like, "Ok, your funeral."

Seeking assurance, I called my mom and dad on the painful drive home. My mom was endlessly sympathetic. My dad, also a self-sufficient warrior who considered the health care industry an evil to be avoided at all costs, agreed with my decision.

"I don't blame you," he said. "I wouldn't let anyone stick a needle in my back! Let's just hope this thing heals on its own." If nothing else I was glad for the validation.

Out of Character

But my gladness didn't last long. That evening after popping pain meds and knocking back several strong drinks, I became so despondent that I just wanted to crawl in bed and sleep. I never made it. As I lifted my leg to slide on to the bed, I misjudged the distance, lost my balance, and crashed to the floor... right on my tailbone. "*UUUUARGH!*"

Writhing in pain, seething in anger, I barked every profane word in the language as I tried and failed to pull myself up. Then I had the sudden thought I was being divinely punished and shouted, "WHY GOD?! Why ME? What did I do to deserve this? Why are you punishing ME?"

Then the gravity of my dire situation sank in, and in a totally-out-of-character act of surrender I pleaded with God to help me. "Please heal me, God. PLEASE have mercy on me. I'm begging you! I'll do anything." Of the couple times I had prayed in my life, that was easily the most desperate.

Totally resigned to defeat and unable to fix myself for the first time in my adult life, I yanked a blanket and pillow from the bed and fell asleep on the floor. I was officially at rock bottom and fearful my life as I knew it was over.

The next morning, I woke up in debilitating pain again and wondered if God had even heard my prayer. Then, only a few minutes after I labored to get to my feet, my phone rang. I was going to push it to voicemail until I saw it was an old friend named James, whom I hadn't talked to in a while. He was always encouraging, and I was in need of encouragement, so I was moved to answer.

"You've been on my mind a lot lately," said James in his familiar pastoral tone, "and something told me I should check up on you. Is everything OK?"

When I told him I injured my back and was going crazy because it refused to heal, he replied, "Oh man you should've called me! You'll never guess what I'm doing for a living now."

"Uh, pharmaceuticals hopefully?" I quipped.

"Nope, I'm a certified massage therapist! Why don't you come down to my new office and let me work on your back?"

Work on my back? Yikes. I pictured him driving his elbow into my spine and putting me in a pain coma. "Thanks, but maybe it will get better soon," I said.

"Don't risk it," he cautioned. "Massage therapy jumpstarts the healing process in ways other therapies and drugs can't. And anyway, what do you have to lose? Don't think about how you'll feel if it fails, think about how you'll feel if it works!"

His optimism was uplifting, and I couldn't deny his point: I was out of options and had nothing to lose. I finally surrendered and agreed to meet him.

Revival

I don't even know how I drove myself downtown and walked two city blocks to his office. It had to be on God's strength because I couldn't even sit down in the lobby as I waited for him. Ten minutes later I was face down on a massage table, cursing myself for coming, and feeling ridiculously vulnerable and pitiful.

In stark contrast, as meditative music flowed out of a small speaker next to a flickering candle, James was as peaceful as a Sunday morning summer breeze. "Now just totally relax and take deep breaths," he gently encouraged me.

Then came a miracle. The second his fingers began slowly kneading my knotted muscles, my whole body decompressed in a sigh of collective relief, followed by a profound sense of relaxation I had never known. I recalled my desperate prayer to God the night before and wondered if He was at that moment answering it.

As the session continued, James inquired about my fitness practices. I told him my life was filled with endless stress, and exercise was my only outlet to purge it. I also expressed anger at myself for having lifted too much weight and getting injured... again. His reply was mind blowing.

"Some injuries are from acute trauma like a sudden car accident, but others are from years of neglect," he counseled. "Picture a slow-motion car accident where the damage accumulates over time until it reaches a failure point. Muscles need to be nourished, conditioned, rested, and strengthened... or they fatigue, weaken, and fail."

I had never heard such a compelling explanation of how muscles worked and shuddered at the possibility that I had ignorantly been doing exercise wrong my whole life. I also had the thought that it was a divine teaching that applied to far more than muscle wellness—like relationships.

Completely sold on the miracle of massage, I made another appointment with the receptionist before I left. Despite several efforts to get him to reconsider, James wouldn't accept any money from me. Then to my amazement I walked back to my car without any excruciating pain. It was a true miracle, and I cried tears of joy and prayed to God again.

A few massage sessions later, with the aid of daily stretching and core strengthening, miraculously my back pain decreased, and my range of motion began to slowly return. Soon I was able to get off anti-inflammatory meds, return to my job search, and even take short walks. I couldn't help but think God had answered my prayers.

Blah, Blah, Blah

Eager to share the healing miracle with someone, I was moved to call a former coworker and Christian minister friend named Aaron. We didn't have a close relationship, but we had discussed spiritual matters in the past (often times to contest each other's opposing theological views), so I was interested to hear his impressions. Moreover, he was the only person I knew who wouldn't think I had gone bat wing mad.

After I told him about my divorce, back injury, and amazing recovery he said, "Hey sorry to hear about your divorce, but praise God for healing. Sometimes God allows us to fall into darkness because that's the only way

He can get our attention to lead us to the *real* healer, Jesus Christ."

Oy. Don't get me wrong, the validation was great, but his sanctimonious implication that I was so lost that God needed to crush me with 300 pounds of industrial steel to get me to *Jesus* was condescending at best. After the call ended, I wondered why he couldn't just be happy for me without all the preachy Jesus stuff. *Blah, blah, blah,* I sighed.

Next, I shared my belief that God had healed my back with my parents. My mom was delighted. My dad, not so much. Of course he was happy for my recovery and congratulated me for my endurance, but glossed over the part about God answering my prayers. I think that was the first time I realized he didn't have a strong sense of spirituality, and it had an unsettling effect on me.

At any rate, though I was thankful to be back on my feet, I still couldn't play basketball or lift weights, and that meant I couldn't vent my deepening divorce angst and separation anxiety from not seeing my kids... and that was completely unknown territory.

On the outside I played the warrior role and talked the *hoowa!* talk, but on the inside all kinds of dark, foreboding fears and aggressions had begun to take root and multiply. With nowhere else to turn, I turned to the bottle and weed to drown them out.

Reflections

The weightlifting fiasco was a painful and humiliating lesson but looking back I'm thankful for it. Not only did it break my prideful will and move me to submit to God (and a healer), but it open my eyes ever so slightly to see the danger of pillaring my life and hope on things that were subject to vanish at the drop of a hat (or a barbell).

It also led me to eye-opening discussions with my dad and Aaron. Finding myself in the middle of their two extreme points of view caused me to consider where I stood on the spiritual side of things and what I believed… which I had never stopped to consider before.

Most importantly, the miraculous healing, combined with the skills and wisdom of James, humbled me greatly and made me realize for the first time that I wasn't the wise, self-sufficient, invincible warrior I thought I was. And that tiny bit of open-mindedness would be critical for what was coming next.

The *Last* Breakup

3: Divine Invitation

"Many are the plans in a person's heart, but it is the LORD'S purpose that prevails." -Proverbs 19:21 (NIV)

Rebecca: As Mark nursed his latest injury, I was celebrating my new freedom. When people expressed condolences about the divorce, I told them it was a *good* thing, and I was over it. Though I still felt anxiety about the future, I was sick and tired of being sick and tired, and I believed every voice (whether it was from a rebellious song or a friend) that assured me I deserved to be happy.

Rolling down my exciting new road to new life and happiness, I was networking, reconnecting with old friends, meeting new people, and trying to get as far away from my "old life" as possible. I was greatly hopeful that I was finally positioned to reach the greener grass I had always dreamt about.

In hindsight I have to laugh because I had no idea where the road was actually going. I was just glad it *seemed* to be going in a direction other than crazy... for once.

Heart Tug

Then the road took an unexpected turn one day when my daughter asked me if she and her brother could go to a youth group at a church called Grace Heart Church. Having never been involved in a church before (other than occasional mass-going with Mark), I hesitated. But after

29

meeting a few of the other kids and their parents, I felt a tug in my heart and decided to let them go.

A few weeks later the road took another turn when one of the kids' moms invited us to attend church service. If it was a rigid and formal church I would have declined because I wasn't in the mood to be reminded of how much of a sinner I was. But this church seemed welcoming to all and even inspirational, so I decided to try it.

Nevertheless, when we pulled into the parking lot Sunday morning my mind wandered with all kinds of questions: *Will there be a welcoming committee? Will it be all weird and awkward? Will people be judgy and preachy? Will they look down on me for divorcing?* I almost turned around and went home.

Thank God I didn't leave, because when we walked through the doors, we were greeted by warm-hearted people who welcomed us like old friends and made us feel totally at home. It was like a homecoming, to a home I had never been to before.

The next thing I knew, we were standing in the worship center, singing along with the most uplifting songs about God's love I ever heard. I didn't know if it was a placebo effect or what, but I could have sworn I felt a deep, reassuring love in my heart, and it filled me with a sense of belonging and worth.

Next up was the pastor's sermon. I was only passively listening at first, but when he began gently preaching about "trusting God with all of your cares and fears," especially when facing difficult trials and worries, I felt another tug on my heart and listened intently.

Then he read from the Bible. It was a passage from the Gospel of Matthew I had never heard:

"Therefore I tell you, do not worry about your life... Look at the birds of the air; they do not sow or reap or store away in barns, and yet your heavenly Father feeds them. Are you not much more valuable than they? Can any one of you by worrying add a single hour to your life?... *But seek first his kingdom and his righteousness*, and all these things will be given to you as well. Therefore do not worry about tomorrow, for tomorrow will worry about itself. Each day has enough trouble of its own." -Matthew 6:25-34 (NIV)

The pastor concluded, "If you obey God first in every part of your life—first, not second or third or fourth, but *first*—He will provide for all your needs, ease your worries, quiet your fears, and give you true worth and value that the world and people cannot give. God's never-failing love will strengthen your faith to get you through difficult trials without toxic dependencies and even heal your heartbreak."

When I heard those words, my heart swelled with hope and my eyes filled with tears. I cried even more when we sang the final song about how God's grace "meets us where we are," and how Jesus embraces and provides for everyone who turns to Him and repents.

Following the service, I mingled with some attendees and was amazed by how kind and welcoming they were. There was no weirdness or judgement at all; just people who loved God and supported each other.

Most surprising, I met married couples and was in awe of how happy and harmonious they seemed. I didn't know if their friendships were genuine, but if nothing else they gave me a tiny bit of hope that happy marriage was somehow possible.

That week I thought about everything I heard at church. Gradually I came to see why the sermon made me cry. I was crying tears of joy. When I heard Jesus welcomed me into His arms and didn't care about my messy past or heavy baggage, I realized I finally found the true love my heart had been searching for. It was the first time I felt fully accepted, loved, and like my life mattered and had a purpose—even though I couldn't fully see the purpose yet.

After that I started attending church regularly. I also decided to start learning how to put God first and "submit to Him in all my ways" because I soon realized I had no idea what that meant.

Helpless Surrender

Several weeks later, I was driving home from work when I noticed new condos being built near the house I was renting. After I did a walkthrough (and fell in love), I decided to roll the dice and apply for a loan. I was shocked when I got approved. Eagerly counting the days until escrow closed, I anxiously looked forward to owning something that was finally *all mine.*

On the day I moved in I was on top of the world. Then disaster struck.

While my brother and I were awkwardly trying to squeeze my sofa through the doorway of my new condo, I suddenly felt a stabbing pain in my lower back that caused me to drop the sofa and scream in agony. I hoped it was just a slight muscle pull; but as the day wore on, and I couldn't even lift a table lamp without horrible pain, I knew it was bad.

With each passing day the pain worsened to the point that I was forced to go on disability and send the kids to Mark's house. He was even more unhappy about my injury than I had been about his. Then bad turned to worse when my employer abruptly let me go because I had only been employed a little while, and they had no obligation to hold my job.

Needless to say, all of my progress, good times, and even church-going had screeched to a halt, and I was devastated. In the past I wouldn't have known where to turn, maybe lost hope, maybe even had a breakdown.

But by the grace of God the Biblical teachings I heard in church about submitting were still fresh in my heart. So, one night while laying helpless on my sofa I prayed, "I surrender to you God. I can't do this by myself. I'm weak and need your strength and courage. Please heal me." I gave it all to Him... all I had left... which admittedly wasn't much.

Under the Knife

After that night, I continued to lean on God in prayer. But while my faith strengthened, my back pain only worsened. It got so bad that I had to stay with my mom.

Thank God she was there for me; I don't know what I would've done without her. She was adamant I see a doctor, so I finally gave in and made an appointment.

After several additional appointments, multiple tests, and a week under the influence of prescription drugs that made me sick and caused hallucinations, the prognosis finally came. The doctor informed me that due to a spinal defect that had been exacerbated by the injury, there was no other option but surgery. I was devastated and scared, but I held firm to my new faith in God and believed in my heart He would protect me.

A couple days later I was being prepped to go under the knife. The last thing I remember before falling asleep was praying to God to restore me to good health. I remember hearing—more like sensing—a voice from deep within assuring me that everything would be OK. I breathed a restful sigh of relief because I knew God was with me.

When I woke from surgery, miraculously the excruciating pain was mostly gone. The surgery appeared to have been a success. After only a brief hospital stay, I miraculously walked out on my own power. I felt like I had been given a new life. I cried tears of joy and thanked God repeatedly.

But gratitude wasn't the only thing I was feeling. Being bed-ridden gave me a lot of time to reflect on what led up to the injury, and soon I was reliving the most toxic scenes from our marriage and feeling deep resentment towards Mark.

If he had been a good husband, I wouldn't have been moving in the first place! I fumed. It wasn't long before I blamed him for my back injury, my job loss, and for having to start over again halfway through life. I couldn't believe I stayed married to him as long as I did. *Grrrrr.*

Moving On

Thankfully I had family and friends who persuaded me not to let my past spoil my future. They coached me to move on and just be happy I finally got the gorilla off my back. My girlfriends made me vow to never put myself back on the crazy train with Mark again. I was glad to oblige.

Soon I was back on my feet and attending church. A few friends I had made there said they had prayed for my recovery. I was surprised because no one other than a few close family members had ever prayed for me before. Their kindness and empathy were like warm soup for my weary soul.

A week later I landed a great job in the real estate industry. It was then I realized my tiny faith in God was leading to friendships, healing, courage, and empowerment, and that made me long for an even greater spiritual connection with Him.

With that said, I had no desire to translate what I was learning about submitting to God to my dead marriage. Even though I had begun to feel a little guilt about divorcing (especially when I was around other couples at church), I didn't let it bother me. I figured if I was partly to blame for our marriage failure, I was fully justified because Mark had never treated me like I thought I deserved to be treated.

Determined to put it all behind me and move on, I began dating and made no apologies for it.

Reflections

I'm a witness to the truth of the scripture at the beginning of this chapter about how God's purpose always prevails. I had all kinds of plans and purposes about how *I* would attain the happiness I was seeking for myself. I never dreamed that with a single "yes" God would lead me to a church where I would experience joy and hope that didn't come from the pleasure of getting what I wanted, but the word and Spirit of God in my heart.

I was deeply moved by how welcoming, accepting, and kind the Grace Heart church members were. They embraced me with the same kindness the pastor said Jesus embraces His new flock members. I don't think I could have come to know God's love as I did without encountering it in the hearts of His family members. Truly, I knew they were Christians by their love, and I wanted to be one of them.

Thankfully God's purpose prevailed, because without my new faith in Him and the prayers of my friends at church, I don't know how I would have made it through my back injury and surgery. It goes to show God knows what we need long before we even know we need it. I'm a witness.

4: Goodwill Treasures

"For the word of God is living and active, sharper than any two-edged sword... discerning the thoughts and intentions of the heart." -Hebrews 4:12 (ESV)

Mark: Though I tried to mentally prepare for it, I was still rattled when I learned Rebecca was dating. That, coupled with a mutual friend's report that she was "as happy as I've ever seen her," stung more than a little. Part of the sting was from anger that she was on the fast track to happy while I was still licking my wounds; the other part was from her flippancy about it. At least that's why I *thought* it stung.

One day when she dropped the kids off at my house, I asked her how she could act like our marriage never even happened. She shrugged and said, "I choose not to live in the past, you should try it," and sped off. I couldn't believe how unapologetically cold she had become.

Rebecca: That's what I said to avoid a blowout, but in truth I was just much happier without him. I could finally live by own terms and rules, and I was free. To put it bluntly I was everything I could never be in our grueling, ball and chain marriage.

Seeking Relief

Mark: On the extreme opposite side of the happy scale, I was struggling to rehab myself back to full health and enduring endless rejections from the jobs I was applying for. Though I played the resilient warrior role to keep up appearances, under my prideful shell I was beset by all kinds of anxieties and a deepening fear that without an outlet for my aggressions I would totally lose it.

Finding no relief from the toxic spirits I had turned to, I finally turned back to God and asked Him to help me find a job and lift me out of the dark place I was sinking into. I had never prayed for such things before. I wasn't even sure if God was listening or cared. I just had a spark of hope that He helped me before, so maybe He would help me again.

As if on cue, within a few days an old friend named Alyssa called. She was a kind and highly intelligent person, but she was also a conversationalist, and I loathed the idea of talking about my divorce drama. Then again, she was well connected in the business world, and I was in desperate need of a job lead, so I decided to pick up.

"How have you been?" she asked warmly. "I haven't heard from you in a while. Is everything OK?" Strangely, it was almost an exact duplicate of the call from my massage therapist friend James.

"I've seen better days, but I'm getting by," I demurred.

"Sorry to hear that, so do you want to talk about it?"

Ugh. No, I didn't want to talk about it. But on further thought, I sort of did, because without a way to purge I felt like a powder keg about to explode. "Uh, well, I'm getting uh... divorced... so yeah... it's crazy right now... but I'm working through it."

"Oh, I'm so sorry to hear that," she sympathized. "How are you feeling about it?"

Ordinarily I wouldn't have answered. In my world, *real men* only talked about how they *thought,* never about how they *felt.* "Facts not feelings" was my mantra. But alas, my world was getting me nowhere fast, so I decided to open up a tiny bit.

"Uh, let's just say I'm not in the best state of mind right now," I confessed. "I injured my back, still can't exercise, my mind's been going a million miles an hour... just feeling kind of down... sort of like a perfect storm."

"Hmm, sorry to hear that," she sympathized. "Hey, have you heard about something called *mindfulness*?"

"Yeah, isn't that some new age guru mind conditioning stuff?" I scoffed.

"No, it's a Zen meditation technique to identify negative thought patterns. It really helps people stop regretting the past and worrying about the future. Sort of like a *mind over matter* type thing. I can send you a copy of a really good book about it if you want?"

Wow, it sounded like the cure for my exact situation. *What do I have to lose?* I wondered. *And anyway, how hard could a little meditation be?* Excited by the possibility I had found the magic elixir to get me out my sunken state, I decided to accept her offer,

When the book arrived in the mail I dove in and started skimming to get to the "meat" (as was my impatient custom). Then I spotted the potential magic:

"Sit still, relax, breathe deep, focus only on your breathing and the rising of your chest. Then, as negative thoughts emerge, ignore them and continue to focus on your breathing..."

Piece of cake, I said to myself. Then I sat on the floor and closed my eyes. *Breathe... breathe... breathe... breathe*—but nope. Not a chance. Trying to stop the raging torrent of negative thoughts that came flying at me was like standing in the middle of a river and trying to stop the water from flowing. I quit on the spot and vowed to never attempt it again.

Sight for Sore Eyes

But the Zen book wasn't a total loss. Though I was done with the meditation part of it, I was still captivated by the author's underlying theory that my depression was just a by-product of negative thought patterns, and soon became determined to figure out how to purge them from my mind.

I headed to the used books section of the local Goodwill Store in hopes of finding a cure. Rifling through the shelves I grabbed every one-dollar book that even resembled a self-improvement book and bought an armful without even skimming them.

Back home I randomly grabbed the first book and opened it. To my surprise it was written by a Christian pastor who claimed the number one, most important thing a person could do to overcome anger, pessimism, fear, anxiety, and much more was to recondition their mind by reciting uplifting and positive... drum roll... *Bible verses?*

Wait. Bible verses?? Wow, what an unorthodox and heretical idea Though I hadn't gone to church regularly since I was young, I still had a firm religious belief that only authorized clergy had permission to give Biblical instruction to people. In my judgment, anyone else who propped themselves up as a Biblical authority of any sort was an imposter—or a fanatic.

Then again, the timing of the book was uncanny given my recent emergency calls to God, so I decided I should at least skim it before writing it off as pseudo-religious quackery. Imagine my shock when my sore eyes were suddenly filled with soul-soothing, uplifting, triumphant Biblical words I couldn't recall hearing before such as:

"If God be for us, who can be against us?"
-Romans 8:31

And...

"ALL THINGS are possible to him who believes."
-Mark 9:23 (NKJV)

And...

"The Lord is my strength and my shield, my heart trusts in Him and He helps me." -Psalm 28:7 (NIV)

And...

"With faith as small as a mustard seed you can move mountains, and nothing will be impossible for you."
-Matthew 17:20 (NIV)

And...

"I can do ALL THINGS through Christ who strengthens me." -Philippians 4:13 (NKJV)

My jaw hit the floor. First, I had been churched most of my childhood and couldn't recall ever hearing such empowering and galvanizing calls to victory before. Moreover, I couldn't get my mind around the idea that God wanted to help me conquer the challenges in my little insignificant life. Strangely it was the most appalling yet revolutionary idea I had ever heard.

Then came the familiar scoffing voice of my inner cynic saying, *Let me get this right: This self-help guru pastor guy is proposing that God, the Creator of the Universe, will help you, average Joe nobody, with your stupid first world problems, simply because you believe in Him and He loves you?? Bahahahaha! I thought you knew God only helps those who help themselves!*

But yet! Right there in front of my eyes were the words of the Bible and multiple testimonies affirming God's power and willingness to help *all* of His children. Scripture after scripture, page after page, it was like a buffet of spiritual food for every life challenge and defeated mindset imaginable—including mine.

Angry? Read this verse. *Sad?* Read that verse. *Fearful?* Read this verse. *Broken-hearted?* Read that verse. *Hopeless?* Read this verse." And the author didn't seem to be endorsing self-help, he was endorsing God's help. And according to him, God's help was available to anyone who affirmed His promises with faith.

Torn between my seasoned cynicism and the promise of what appeared to be personalized, supernatural help, I decided to sleep on it. But that evening something unexpected happened: I felt uplifted and even a little hopeful... and was perfectly sober. I assumed I would feel different the next day. But in the morning I felt just as good… and remarkably even energized. *Wow.*

Eager to find out if it was just a fluke or I was onto something life-changing, in a rare act of defiance against my own doubt I wrote some of the verses on little cards and put them in my wallet, as the author prescribed. Then, every time I had a negative or self-defeating thought, I read one or more of the verses aloud. Initially I felt self-conscious and even foolish at times, but then something astonishing happened.

The more I declared verses like, "If God is for me who can be against me?" the more I believed them. Then lo and behold, a short while later three seemingly miraculous things happened. First, I had a much more positive mindset and even felt some of my confidence return. Then I landed a great job. Then a prominent media company agreed to sell a music keyboard learning manual I had pitched to them months earlier. It was a miracle.

Unvalidated

A part of me wanted to celebrate. But alas, another part of me, the dogmatic part that questioned the authority of some pastor guy to interpret the will of God and the power of God's word to positively impact my life, was still very skeptical.

Ever the skeptic, I decided to call my dad for a second opinion. Owing to an eight-book-a-month reading habit, he was a walking library of knowledge (not to mention an interminable critic), and I was sure he'd have a lot to say on the matter.

To my surprise he didn't have much to say at all. After hearing my spirited testimony, he only dryly opined, "Well, I believe God only helps those who help themselves, but to each his own." Funny, I felt the same way initially.

Given my respect for his knowledge (not to mention a lifelong quest for his approval), ordinarily I might have agreed with him. But judging by his indifferent answer he didn't seem too informed on the subject, so I decided to look elsewhere for validation. That was also a first.

Next, I called my friend Aaron again. Despite his annoying evangelistic overtures, he was a staunch proponent of "living by the word of God," and I was sure he'd approve of my new Biblical therapy. But nope.

After hearing my testimony, he rambled, "God's word is living and active, and it has power to uplift, but the main purpose of the Bible is to lead people to Jesus and teach them..." *blah, blah, blah*. Not what I wanted to hear. I made an excuse and told him I had to go.

In the past, without validation I might have been deflated and maybe even wrote my blessings off to dumb luck. But over the next few days something strange happened again. My belief in the power of God's word only intensified, and soon I became so hungry to learn more that I went back to the Goodwill store and bought my first Bible.

Upon returning home I placed the red Bible on a table next to my sofa and vowed to read a little daily. I figured the more verses I learned, the sooner I would be able to recondition my chaotic mind and finally put my past—and

Rebecca—behind me for good. That was *my* big plan anyway.

Reflections

Once again came the love of a friend (Alyssa) immediately after praying. Though I didn't take to meditating, the gift she sent me was an important development for a couple reasons. First, it awoke me to what a mess my mind had become (not to mention my inability to sit still). Second, it compelled me to keep seeking answers, which led me to the Bible verse book and ultimately a Bible. I think it goes to show God uses everything and everyone to light the way to the Truth.

That said I'd be remiss if I didn't add that the only reason I accepted help was because I believe God had given me the will to listen, learn, and even open up after I prayed to Him. Without that new willingness, I would have pridefully declined Alyssa's offer, just as I was tempted to do when James offered his help.

More importantly, discovering God's word in such a personal and uplifting form outside formal religion was a major blow to my dogmatic worldview. The possibility of a personal God and Savior who really cared about my little life never even dawned on me until I read those verses.

I didn't consciously perceive it, but after defiantly going against the voices of doubt (including the voice of my own inner cynic), I had begun to follow a new voice for the first time.

For good measure, while to this day I believe the living and active word of God has real transformative power, and that God uses every word for his purposes (Isaiah 55:11 affirms this), I've also learned—as Aaron alluded to—God's word indeed has a much greater purpose than improving mindsets and building confidence. I just hadn't yet come to see it.

Another thing I hadn't yet come to see was that the mental torment I was trying to purge from my mind was actually rooted in my soul.

5: Faith Leaping

"Have I not commanded you? Be strong and courageous. Do not be frightened, and do not be dismayed, for the LORD your God is with you wherever you go." -Joshua 1:9 (NKJV)

Rebecca: With my back finally on the mend, I was excited to return to my new, liberated life. I had no idea what the future held, but learning God's many promises about His unfailing friendship, love, and protection gave me a new sense of gratitude and hope. It was in that spirit that I began seeking ways to give back at church.

Divine Invitation

I got my chance one evening when I picked up the kids from youth group. As I waited out front for them, one of the youth group leaders named Sarah jogged out and asked if I had a minute to talk. She said my daughter had suggested I might be interested in volunteering to be a chaperone at an upcoming... *youth group retreat??*

I froze. *Me? Mentor? Really?* I had never been in any sort of official leadership role before, plus I knew very little about the Bible. *What if I made a complete fool of myself? What if I misled people?*

Sarah must have sensed my fears. "Don't worry if you don't have experience," she assured me, "the ministers will be doing all the teaching. We just need you to keep an eye on the kids and reinforce what they're learning. I'll be right there with you, and plus you'll learn a lot."

I immediately felt another huge tug on my heart and knew I couldn't resist. "I've never done anything like this," I confessed, "and I'm really new to the church, but sure, I'd love to go."

She was ecstatic. *"Really?* That would be such an amazing blessing. We've actually been praying because if we couldn't find someone today, we were going to have to cancel the retreat. I can't thank you enough. I'll email you the details. Don't worry, you'll be *great!* God bless you, Rebecca."

That night I replayed our conversation in my mind. I was in awe of how encouraging Sarah had been and blown away by how God—it had to be God, I thought—called me up to be the answer to their prayers. *Me! A baby in the faith, with no experience at all!*

I shared my anxiety with a friend at church. She said, "Don't worry, God doesn't call the qualified, He qualifies the called. You'll be just fine." Admittedly it was hard to comprehend God wanted to qualify little old *me* to do anything for Him, but it felt right, and I believed it.

When I told Mark we were going to the retreat he wasn't happy. At the time, he still believed his religious denomination was the only "legit church" and wouldn't entertain any other possibilities. But I had new confidence to stand firm, so much to Mark's chagrin I told him my mind was made up—and there was nothing he could do to change it.

Thank God I decided to go; it would turn out to be the second most transformative experience of my life.

Pride Walls

The theme of the camp was "Take God Everywhere." It was filled with Bible-themed talks, games, challenges, and open discussion. Each one reinforced the power of God through Jesus Christ to save, heal, and restore broken hearts and broken people. There were quite a few kids who came from broken homes, and I got really emotional when I realized I was clinging to every teaching as much as they were.

Over dinner I chatted with one of the ministers and learned how untreated heart wounds cause people to erect defensive walls of pride around their hearts. "Pride prevents God's love from entering our hearts," he said, "and that's a problem because only God's love can heal our wounds and produce true forgiveness, healing, and reconciliation."

I thought of all the painful baggage I carried from my marriage and said, "I don't see how it's possible to get over all the pain from my past." I can still hear his reply today. "It's not possible without submission to Jesus, but with Jesus anything is possible."

That evening during quiet time, I had an epiphany that my "baggage" was actually heart wounds from all the disappointment and pain I had endured, and that maybe my own pride walls had prevented God's love from entering my heart and healing it.

Feeling really emotional again, I couldn't help but wonder if maybe God had brought me to the retreat to help me submit to Jesus so He could heal my heart wounds. The only problem was, the idea of opening my heart was very uncomfortable, and I had no idea how to submit yet. I barely even knew a word of the Bible.

Thankfully, in the morning breakfast talk the pastor helped me understand my struggle. He taught how submitting requires repenting and opening our hearts for the Holy Spirit to enter (to bring forth the truth so we can be healed and grow closer to God), but how that can be scary for some people because it requires vulnerability, and vulnerability requires something many people don't have, and that's TRUST. Oh.

Then he said, "Repenting and trusting God the Father with our hearts is hard for a lot of reasons. One of the reasons is pride, another is fear, especially if we've suffered a lot of heartbreak… even in childhood. We need God's courage to trust Him to heal our hearts."

Ouch. When he said that, my heart stirred, and I felt a shiver of sadness. Flashing back briefly on my painful childhood, I couldn't help but wonder if I was still carrying unhealed wounds from it.

Then one of the young ladies raised her hand and asked, "So how do we get better at trusting God and having faith in Him?"

The pastor answered, "Faith comes from submission to Jesus, repentance, hearing God's word in our ears and hearts. But even after God gives us faith, we still have to let go, take the leap of faith and trust Him. Good news! We're going to let go and take some faith leaps together today to get a feel for it."

Then we went faith leaping. To help us overcome our fears of letting go and trusting God, we did physical challenges such as "the trust fall," where you stand on a platform, fold your arms, and fall backwards into the arms of fellow campers. We also did the "faith leap," where you climb high up a tree in a harness and literally let go and leap from one platform to another.

Looking back, I'm still in awe of my courage to climb 50 feet up a Redwood tree, let go, and jump—especially considering my back wasn't fully healed. But in retrospect, I know it wasn't my strength or courage holding me up; it was God's hand. It was only from surrendering and putting all my trust in Him that I was able to "let go."

Third Day

The highlight of the camp was the third and last day when we were given a chance to submit to Jesus, repent, and pledge to follow Him. Prior to the camp, I was learning about Jesus, but it wasn't until that day I realized He was, as one of the leaders said, "the only way of truth, the only way to receive the gift of eternal life, and the only way to be one in God's love."

When the pastor asked who was ready to give their life to Jesus, I didn't know exactly what I was getting into when I was moved to raise my hand. But when people started walking to the front, I took another leap of faith and joined them.

Then I was standing in front of the pastor, at the base of the stairway to heaven, confessing:

"Dear Jesus, I ask for your forgiveness and repent of my sins. I surrender my life to you as my Lord and Savior. I can't do this life on my own. I invite you into my heart to heal my wounds, lead me, teach me, and be the rock of truth in my life forever."

I knew instantly it was the best decision I ever made. As I floated back to my seat, I felt lighter than a feather, beautiful, accepted, validated, and immeasurably worthy. There wasn't a dry eye in the room—including mine and my son and daughter's. I've learned being in the presence of the Holy Spirit has that effect on people.

On my way home from the camp, I called my mom to tell her about the weekend. I cried tears of joy because I felt like a massive hole in my heart had been filled. I testified that surrendering to Jesus was like going to the doctor's office with an incurable disease and being told there was a new cure. That was my very first testimony about Jesus Christ.

Here's a passage I wrote in my journal that night:

"I have committed to following Jesus. I commit to seeking Him daily and learning to trust God as my Father in every way. I've thrown out all of my dirty music, less-than-modest clothing, and inappropriate movies that I felt were poor examples for my kids and not helpful in my faith walk. I'm also going to select my friends more carefully. I have made the decision to follow Jesus."

Tug of War

The following week, I took another faith leap when I accepted an invitation from my new friend Sarah (the lady who invited me to the camp) to attend a Women's Bible Study. It was not only a leap because I had never been encouraged to learn as a child (and had a lifelong phobia of learning), but also because the majority of the women in attendance were married.

Shortly after the meeting started, it didn't take long to realize how much the women in attendance loved God and His word. Even more amazing was how openly and lovingly they talked about their marriages and husbands—rather than with jokes, put-downs, or complaints. I felt like I had stepped into the twilight zone.

We talked about many life challenges that were surprisingly common to all of us, such as the desire to gossip, being emotionally-driven, and the desire to be in control all the time, all of which opposed God's will. We also talked about forgiveness, and I was surprised to learn I wasn't the only one who struggled with it.

The leader affirmed what I learned at the retreat when she said, "Power to overcome temptation, not to mention forgiveness and healing, only happen when we open our hearts to the Holy Spirit. But in order for the Holy Spirit to be in our hearts we must trust God, and that includes obeying Christ's commands (John 14:15).

Back to trust again. *Trust, trust, trust*, that was the message I was receiving loud and clear. I was glad when the closing prayer was all about receiving the courage to trust God. I needed it.

It was an exciting time of faith leaps, discovery, and renewal, but soon I found myself facing a new problem. The more I trusted God and opened my heart, the more resentment I felt towards Mark for neglecting me and our marriage for so long.

It was a deep, agonizing resentment unlike any I had ever felt, and it brought back painful memories that I had totally forgotten about. Then came a tug of war between my desire to trust God and my desire to get out of the emotional pain from my old life.

Unfortunately, the desire to get out of pain prevailed, and I started hanging out with old friends and going out at night. Under the influence of numbing spirits, it didn't take long to start feeling better and vowing to party like there was no tomorrow when the divorce was final. At that point, I assumed I was "out of the woods" and over my past. Me and my assumptions.

Reflections

Giving my life to Jesus at the retreat is the number one, most important thing I've ever done. Though I still had a lot of uncomfortable truths to face and bridges to cross, it was the day that I took the first step to truly let go and surrender my heart and control, to trust Jesus as my Lord and Savior, rather than myself or anyone else.

Until I attended the camp, I never thought about Jesus in terms of taking away my heavy burdens of doubt, fears, anxiety, stress, insecurities, etc. But when I learned the Scripture in which He says "Come to me all of you who are weary and burdened, and I will give you rest" in Matthew 11:28 (NIV), I gained an all new perspective and respect for His power to heal and restore people—including me—to new life.

The only problem was, I wanted to skip the next part of the Scripture that reads, "take my yoke upon you and learn [the truth] from me." Why? Because the truths God was revealing to me were all tied to my past… which I was desperately trying to move on from.

Once again, the road to my new life had bent in an unexpected direction to a spiritual destination I never could have fathomed. Little did I know God was training me for a much greater challenge than climbing a tree.

The *Last* Breakup

6: Surprise Party

"But now trouble comes to you, and you are discouraged; it strikes you, and you are dismayed." -Job 4:5 (NIV)

Mark: After witnessing the power of God's word, landing a new job, and beginning my keyboard learning manual project, I was feeling mentally and physically better. Though I couldn't exercise and hadn't opened my red Bible, I was still reciting Bible verses occasionally, especially as I took longer walks around my neighborhood.

Metaphorically speaking, it seemed like the clouds were finally beginning to part, and for the first time in months the light up ahead didn't appear to be an oncoming train. Finally, I had taken a step forward. Everything seemed to be going great until...

Out of Nowhere

One day a mutual friend was at my house for a barbecue and asked how I was holding up. I proudly reported, "A lot better, thanks to God."

"Well that's good, because your ex is doing great too!"

"Why do you say that?" I asked nervously.

"Oh, because she's throwing a big divorce party!"

Thud! That was the sound of me and my positive mindset falling off cloud nine and crashing to the ground again.

I did my best to conceal my emotions and play it cool, but inside my ego was sizzling like the beef ribs on the grill. I couldn't believe Rebecca's disrespect and callousness. After my friend left, I called her and demanded to know why she would do such a degrading thing as "having a freaking party to celebrate the death of our marriage?!"

At first, she accused me of "prying into her business" and threatened to block me for good. Then I lost it and said she was disrespectful, hypocritical, and that I regretted marrying her. Then she snapped.

"Who are *you* to lecture *anyone* about marriage respect?!" She yelled. "You weren't proud of me or our marriage. You only took pride in yourself. You never gave your heart to our marriage!"

I couldn't believe what I was hearing. "Excuse me??" I roared back. "I didn't give my *heart*? What does that even mean? I gave you money, kids, and a nice house! I gave you *everything*, but you were never happy! You always wanted more, more, more, and nothing was ever good enough!"

Then came the knockout punch. "Yep, you gave me everything—everything except your heart. I've seen how *real* men at my church love their wives and treat them like gold, and I will never settle for second best again."

Real men?! Church?! What the?! I was so staggered and dazed by her sanctimonious accusations that I couldn't find the words to respond......... until she had hung up and it was too late.

Rebecca: I didn't want to fight with Mark. I had been consciously avoiding contact because I knew it would spiral into another blowout. But he caught me off guard with his call, and when he turned the blame gun on me, I reflexively came out swinging. Old habits die hard.

Mark: Pacing in my backyard, I attempted to reconnect multiple times to defend my honor. But after my calls went to voice mail repeatedly, it was clear she had either blocked me or wasn't going to pick up. I tried to deep-breathe myself back to calm. *Breeeeathe, breeeathe.* It wasn't working.

Overheating

Still fuming later that evening, I wondered which was worse: that Rebecca was planning a *divorce party,* that she had accused me of being heartless, or that she said I wasn't a *real man* compared to other men at her so-called church. I couldn't stand not being able to defend myself, and I was mortified that she was probably trashing me to anyone who would listen.

I tried to douse my smoldering anger in drink and smoke, but that only made things worse. So, I did something I had never done before and took to the phone to vent-rant to friends. Puffing cigarettes and pacing again, I growled to one friend, "I can't believe how self-righteous and arrogant she is!"

Having been through a messy divorce himself, he affirmed, "Some women are just plain evil, and you got stuck with one. Just be happy she's out of your life and will be someone else's problem soon. And don't worry about any demons of guilt or regret, you'll learn to live with them."

Ugh. My blood curdled at the thought of living with demons.

Another friend assured me the anger I was feeling was normal in a divorce, so I should just let it roll off my back. "What, did you think divorce would be easy?" he laughed. "False accusations and guilt are part of the process. Just be patient, and in time you'll be golden."

Golden? I couldn't process that word in the crucible of divorce war.

Disheartened by their responses, I called my friend Alyssa (the one who sent me the meditation book). She was always objective. I was sure she would hear my side of the story and validate me. But nope. Instead she threw a curve when she asked, "Why do you suppose Rebecca's still able to get under your skin like this, friend?"

"*What*?! Oh, come on!" I erupted in feigned laughter. "She's not under my skin at *all!* She's just being cruel and hypocritical. Going to church, throwing a divorce party, and dragging my name through the mud? *Seriously?* What a joke. I'm just venting OK? It will pass."

"OK, I understand," she said... although she didn't sound too convinced.

Voices in the Wind

But my anger didn't pass. Soon I had no choice but to concede Rebecca was indeed under my skin, like a deep sliver, and I had no idea how to get her out. Totally exasperated, I threw on my shoes and took off walking, destination unknown.

I ended up at a levee just outside my neighborhood and decided to walk it. Wandering down the lonely road I agonized over Rebecca's shocking and penetrating charges against my character and integrity as a man. She had done plenty of blaming in the past, but she had never accused me of being a user and an imposter. I wanted to dismiss her, but she had been so assertive and confident that I couldn't ignore the disturbing possibility there was a grain of truth to what she said.

Then came the aggravating voice of my conscience wondering, *Was I really that disconnected and selfish? Was I really that much of a... jerk? Or was she just plain evil like my friend suggested?*

With the sun quickly setting and no answers to be found, I decided to turn back and head home.

On the walk back I thought about how quickly my positive mindset had dissolved into anger and loathing upon hearing the dreadful news of Rebecca's party and her accusations. It caused me to wonder if the Biblical verses I had been reading were powerless, and if I had just been imagining God's help.

Then came the voice of my inner cynic again chiding me, *See? God doesn't care about your little life. He's got better things to do than tend to your first world problems. You're on your own, as always. Time to man up!*

It was hard to disagree.

Then, as I leaned into a strong headwind, I became overwhelmed with frustration and yelled, "Why me God? Why can't I just divorce and move on like everyone else? Why am I being hung out to dry??" I listened intently for His answer, but all I heard was the voice of my inner cynic again saying, *God is not listening to you.*

Returning to my neighborhood, I was about halfway down my street when I encountered a couple with a baby stroller. For some reason my eyes were drawn to the man. I noticed how he was smiling warmly and listening with great interest to the woman as she talked, like he would rather be nowhere else in the world.

Suddenly it struck me that Rebecca and I had never shared that kind of engaged, conversational, mature friendship before, nor had I ever been as content to be with her as the man appeared to be with the woman.

Ouch. I felt a sharp pang of guilt in my stomach, followed by the dreadful thought again that maybe, somehow, there was a grain of truth to Rebecca's accusation that I hadn't given enough of my heart in our marriage.

Striving for Peace

Still feeling convicted later that night, I felt an incredibly urgent impulse from my conscience to make peace with Rebecca. Though I was still outraged by her degrading assertion that I wasn't a *real man*, I could at least admit I should have spent more time with her and hopefully ease the new resentment she evidently had towards me. Furthermore, it would be a small price to pay to reclaim my dignity and hopefully get her to relent.

I sent her an email that evening saying, "Dear Rebecca, Though I totally disagree with your opinion that I'm not a real man, I'm sorry I didn't spend more time with you and that you felt slighted. That said, I hope we can move on in peace going forward—including not talking bad about each other or throwing a divorce party. I really did my best with what I knew. Your friend, Mark"

Upon clicking the SEND button, I congratulated myself for taking the "high road." I assured myself everything happens for a reason, and that Rebecca would appreciate my gesture and that would be that. That was the pattern, and the pattern never failed... yet.

Rebecca: I received Mark's apology email but had no desire to reply because I doubted his sincerity. For all I knew he was trying to patch things up again—not so we could clear the air and be friends, but so he didn't have to face the truth about himself. That was his pattern, and I was *never, ever* falling for it again.

If I wanted to throw a divorce party, I would throw one. And after his attack I decided to throw an even bigger one than I originally planned.

Reflections

Mark: Up until that phone call with Rebecca, I was under the belief that the worst crime I was guilty of in our marriage was not giving her more attention. To be sure, she had leveled plenty of other accusations through the years, but never attacked my character and essentially convicted me of being an imposter husband... let alone a less-than-noble Christian *man*. I took immense pride in my character and integrity (not to mention my religious morality, even though I was not exactly "practicing") and was incensed that she was not only undermining my "good name," but probably trashing it to everyone she knew—maybe even my kids.

But as hot as I was, and as much as I doubted and questioned God for my lack of "moving on" progress, I couldn't ignore the convicting voice of my conscience, which nagged me non-stop to consider the merits of Rebecca's accusations (and question why she would be so angry that she felt the need to throw a *party* to be liberated from me). Hence my urgency to make peace with her and put it all behind me.

Only in retrospect can I see that my default setting when confronted with uncomfortable accusation was to "put it all behind me" and "make peace" as soon as possible. I actually thought my passion for making peace quickly was a virtue. I had no clue that I wasn't actually making peace, but only making pain go away temporarily, consistent with my "fix it fast" temperament.

I hadn't yet come to realize that I wasn't actually a peacemaker, but rather—as Rebecca alluded to—a truth and pain dodger. That was the *real* pattern—although my pride blinded me from seeing it.

Alas, I was still convinced there was an evil conspiracy against me. Ironically there was, just not the one I thought.

7: Inconvenient Truths

"When the spirit of truth comes, he will guide you into all truth... and he will declare to you the things that are to come." -John 16:13 (ESV)

Rebecca: After the blowout with Mark, I was feeling better and thought I was out of the woods of resentment and loathing. Though I hadn't really been praying or talking to God much since the retreat, I was still going to church and Bible Study and loved the new story God seemed to be writing for me. Then came an unexpected and inconvenient plot twist.

Divinely Designed

Ever since I started attending church, I heard how obeying God's commands were hard because they often went against our desires. I thought that was odd because I hadn't found anything hard about being a Christian yet. Compared to the crazy train I was on for so many years, it was a walk in the park.

That all changed one night at Women's Bible Study when the leader announced we would be studying— surprise!—"Christian marriage and the divinely designed roles of husbands and wives." *Nooooo. Anything but that*, I thought.

My first reaction was to run for my life. I even leaned over and whispered to a friend, "I don't think this is for me, sorry." But when she encouraged me to stay, saying I could trust God had a purpose for me being there, I felt another tug on my heart and reconsidered.

After an opening prayer and introductions, we read several Bible verses about marriage, specifically the necessity of both husband and wife submitting so they could serve their "divinely-designed" roles, which were evidently necessary for the marriage to be harmonious. Then came this verse, which I had heard before but never liked:

"Wives, submit to your own husbands, as to the Lord. For the husband is head of the wife, as also Christ is head of the church; and He is the Savior of the body. Therefore, just as the church is subject to Christ, so let the wives be subject to their own husbands in everything." -Ephesians 5:22 (NKJV)

Ugh. My internal response was the same as it had always been: *There's no way I'm ever submitting to a man. No one will ever be the "head" of me.*

How did I come to that belief? I grew up in the female empowerment era in which women were encouraged and even pressured to be in charge—of the house, the family, and even the husband. Therefore, I considered myself an "evolved" woman, and like all evolved women, I believed in male-female equality. I didn't think it was right that men should have all the *power*.

It's not that I believed it was impossible to submit to a man; I just didn't believe it was possible for *me*. I just couldn't be a soft, submissive, and trusting type. In my experience, men only cared about one thing, and every time I witnessed another woman weakly "submitting" to a man, it never ended well for her.

On top of all that, I was on the road to new independence and becoming a proud, assertive, and outspoken woman. I couldn't fathom rolling over and submitting to anyone—especially opportunistic men. No. Just no.

But then the Bible Study leader blasted a massive hole in my worldview when she explained that *Biblical* submission doesn't mean being a spineless pushover who bows to her husband's every demand.

"In stark opposition to what the world says," She ministered to us, "The *Biblical* definition of submission is to follow God's will and 'get under, lift up, and put in order' the marriage and family, in harmony with the husband."

That was news to me, but I still didn't understand why all the pressure was on the wife to submit and not the husband. Then came the answer when we read another passage about the role of the husband, in which God commands husbands to not only submit to their wives, but to "love their wives as Christ loves the church and gave Himself up for her." -Ephesians 5:25 (NKJV)

Well blow me over with a feather! The Biblical definition of submission was drastically different than the one I had been taught by the world. I had been led to believe marriage submission was a horrible thing because it degraded and oppressed women, yet here I was learning directly from the Bible that not only was the husband also supposed to submit, but God calls him to a higher submission standard than He calls the wife! *Wow just wow!* I had no idea.

Divine Desire

Still, due to my lifelong conditioning it was hard to imagine a submissive husband who loved His wife as Jesus loves His flock. One thing's for sure: I hadn't met many, including Mark. I wondered how a wife could submit if her husband didn't submit. I decided to ask.

"I'm glad you asked," the leader answered. "God's design for marriage is that both husband and wife submit and obey His commands. If only one submits, the marriage is not harmonious with God's design, and it will be uphill climb. In that case, counseling is needed to figure out why one is not obeying God's commands."

Another lady asked, "What do we do if we can't find the desire to submit?"

The leader answered, "Desire to submit is a fruit of the spirit that comes from God. That's why we are called to submit to God first. Submission brings the power of the Holy Spirit to submit to our husbands, and vice versa. Trying to have a mutually submissive marriage without the power of the Holy Spirit in our hearts is like trying to run a marathon without water."

Wow. I saw a vision of Mark and I slogging up the road of our laborious marriage, dying of thirst, barely hanging on for life, on the verge of collapsing for so many years.

Yep, that was our marriage.

Submission Power

The other ladies in attendance then shared their marriage testimonies. Some were still on their first marriages, some divorced, some remarried. All testified about both the joy of marriage when they and their husbands were submitting and obeying God, and the pain when one or both of them weren't. I definitely related to the pain scenarios.

As an example, one lady shared how her husband had been addicted to porn, and how devastated and small she felt when she found out. But then she submitted, prayed, and drew strength from God to confront the truth with her husband. Miraculously he was driven to repentance and submission, God gave her the power to forgive him and heal, and not only did he overcome his addiction, but they became exponentially closer to God and each other.

She attributed their success to submitting, grace, and faith, and repeated the importance of believing the Bible verse I had been hearing a lot:

"I can do all things through Christ who strengthens me." -Philippians 4:13 (NKJV)

After the testimonies we discussed how the ultimate purpose of marriage is to glorify God, and how only when both spouses submit and have faith does God grant them the *power* to overcome the many challenges of male-female cohabitation, and free them from the exhausting duty of trying to please each other.

She concluded, "Only then can husband and wife live in loving friendship and harmony… and even become a ministry that glorifies God."

Pure twilight zone.

Miraculously, my friend turned out to be right: Even though I wasn't actively married I still learned a lot of insightful things from the Bible Study. Afterwards I wrote two main points in my journal before leaving:

1 Husbands and wives are commanded to submit to each other.

2 Both must first submit to God through Christ to receive the love of the Holy Spirit to harmoniously fulfill their divinely-designed roles in marriage.

Learning Seeds

The only sticking point for me was that due to my life long conditioning and dysfunctional marriage, I still had trouble believing a truly happy, harmonious, and stable marriage was possible... for me.

I shared my doubts with my friend Sarah later. She knew I was divorcing and doing everything I could to move on, so I figured she would validate me. Her response caught me off guard.

She said, "Don't worry, it's totally natural to have doubts about God's way because it's so different than the way of the world. Just remember God teaches with learning seeds, and He will nurture them to fruition later. The important thing is that you keep an open heart, keep seeking, and keep trusting He will reveal the truth and His will at the *perfect moment.*"

I understood what she was saying, but I didn't like the implication that God hadn't revealed the truth and His will to me yet—as if there was a chance our disaster marriage could be saved. My mind was made up that God didn't want me with Mark, and anyone who actually knew my whole situation would agree.

To be sure, Mark was a very independent, prideful man who had never been passionate about being married. I didn't think for a moment he could ever love me like Jesus loves believers. And even if heck froze over and he somehow changed, I didn't think I could ever be in love with him again. Too much baggage. Too much pain. *Never, ever, ever,* I vowed again.

Reflections

Hearing the surprising truth about Christian marriage submission was heartening because it gave me a grain of hope in the possibility of harmonious marriage, which, prior to that Bible Study session, I had lost all hope in.

That said, while I appreciated the teaching and even hoped it was true, it was a hard pill to swallow because it went against my will to divorce, my belief that Mark could never change, and my belief that our marriage couldn't possibly ever be harmonious.

So rather than swallow the pill, I decided to discard it and take more of an "a la carte" approach to my faith. That is, I would keep following the will of God, but only in the areas that worked for me and my way of life. I couldn't yet see that it was impossible to serve two masters.

The *Last* Breakup

8: Who Do You Play For?

"The first to put forth his case seems right, until someone... cross-examines him." -Proverbs 18:17 (ISV)

Mark: When Rebecca didn't respond to my peace offering email, I was left to endlessly brood over her brutal accusations and dread her upcoming divorce party. I would have preferred another knock-down, drag-out battle over the maddening silent treatment. It played tricks on my mind to the extent that I found myself defending my honor to mutual friends without even being prompted. ("I was a good husband! She's lost her mind!")

With my back not healed enough to purge my mounting anguish and increasingly vocal conscience, I decided to try dating, with the hope that meeting new people would get my mind off my troubles so I could move on. When that didn't bring any relief, I reluctantly returned to reciting empowering Bible verses.

But to my great frustration, day after day nothing changed, and soon I was drowning in alcohol again and unsure if God was with me, or far from me. Then, just when all hope seemed lost...

Professor Heart Strings

One day I was working on my keyboard learning manual project and listening to jazz piano to try and relax, when I suddenly felt a strong desire to find a piano coach to raise my self-taught piano skills to the next level.

Yes! Maybe this is just what I need, I coached myself. *Maybe I can finally get my mind off my troubles and even find something new to take pride in. I can reinvent myself!* Suddenly I had a little hope again.

So, I took to Craig's List to find an easy-going piano teacher; not a disciplinarian who would saddle me with a dreadful practice curriculum; just an easy-going coach who would respect my existing skills [I use that term loosely] and provide a *fast track* to success. *Work smarter not harder* was my mantra. I was all about the *fast track.*

Imagine my elation when I came across an ad titled "Learn the Piano at Your Pace." *Boom.* Exactly what I was looking for. In the ad, a guy named Professor Mateo Harper promised a "no fluff" teaching adventure, custom tailored to each player's unique needs. *Sold!* I sent him an email to learn more and anxiously awaited his reply.

Professor Mateo replied quickly. In his email he introduced himself and explained the necessity of "getting to know his potential students" to learn about their specific goals... therefore he was extending me an invitation to meet for... *lunch*??

Admittedly a lunch invite from a stranger made me more than a little suspect about his motives. After all, it was Craig's List, where things weren't always what they seemed. For all I knew the lunch meeting was a pretext for a product demo or sales pitch of some kind.

Nevertheless, after a few more exchanges he seemed credible, so I agreed to meet him at Chili's later in the week. I also told him what I looked like so he could identify me. When I added the meeting to my calendar, I noticed his email address was "Music for the Heart Strings." I hoped he wasn't... weird.

On the day of our lunch meeting my suspicion meter redlined when he strode into the Chili's lobby wearing neon-colored clothing and embraced me in a bear hug like we were long lost brothers separated at birth. I had never been hugged that tightly—especially by a male—and it felt awkward to say the least. I reciprocated with an alligator-armed hug and asked, "So you must be Mateo?"

Taking a step back with a beaming smile he thundered, "Nice to meet you my brother!" Professor Heart Strings was in the house.

As the hostess led us to a table, I was almost certain he was going to talk my ear off for the next hour, and I regretted coming. But every one of my cynical thoughts flew out the window when we sat down and he said, "Mr. Mark my goal is to learn as much as possible about your background and motivations for learning piano. So let's hear it. The stage is yours."

That was music to my ears. I figured the more I told him, the more he would appreciate my background and be moved to fast-track me. I gave him a long rundown of my passion for music, my self-taught piano skills, my artistic endeavors, and how I was currently writing a keyboard learning manual for musicians. I concluded with, "Now I just need a fast-track coach that can help me learn jazz piano."

As I spoke, he listened with intense focus and asked clarifying questions frequently as if he was interviewing me for a job. I assumed he would be impressed by my deep knowledge and experience and tell me we could get started away. But nope. Instead he rambled about how playing jazz "requires deep knowledge, skills, and experience and doesn't lend itself to fast track learning."

Grrr. Exactly what I didn't want to hear.

"Often times students *think* they are ready to play advanced piano due to their backgrounds," he schooled me, "but in reality, they don't have the foundation of piano *fundamentals and principles* to build on and need to take a few steps back before they can start stepping forward."

Sigh. Another step back. Deflated by his wet blanket disclaimer I decided I was probably wasting my time. But after hearing a little more of his music philosophy and being moved by his surprising encouragement, I decided to accept his invite to go to his studio for a "quick demonstration."

Higher Purpose

His studio was a little triangular space in the very back corner of a retail piano store. To get to it we had to weave through a crowd of intimidating grand pianos that sparkled under the bright fluorescent lights and boasted price tags higher than that of the average new car.

In his little corner of the store was an upright piano with a bench, a chair, and an old cabinet with an out-of-place green and red elf figurine on one of its shelves. He sat in the chair and motioned for me to sit on the piano bench. Then he pointed to the piano and said, "Ok let's hear it. The stage is yours." He wanted me to play for him. *Ack.*

I immediately tensed up as I tried to think of something to play. Since I didn't know any songs by heart, I fumbled through a few jazzy-sounding chords I knew and attempted to string them together into a song. Not surprisingly, it didn't come out well, so after an awkward minute I ended my "audition" abruptly and shrugged with a nervous laugh.

To my surprise he seemed pleased and asked if I had written the "song" I just played for him. I laughed, thinking he must be kidding. Seeing he was dead serious, I said, "Uh yeah, just something I made up."

But just as I started feeling confident again, he abruptly launched into a sugarless assessment of my audition in which he observed I was "rigid, shaky, nervous, and unsure of myself..." Then he explained how those problems prevented me from *making a connection* with him as a listener.

Yikes. I wasn't accustomed to that kind of candor, and admittedly it bruised my ego and put me on the defensive. Hoping to salvage a little of my pride I said, "Well, I'm probably just nervous because I don't play much for people."

At that he looked puzzled and asked, "Really? So *who do you play for?"*

Whoa. I had never considered who I played for. I had to think about it before finally answering. "Uh, I guess I just play for myself... is that a bad thing?"

He paused for a few seconds, as if to choose his words carefully. "Well, it's not necessarily a bad thing, I just believe *music is a gift and language of the heart* to share

77

with others, and if we keep it all to ourselves, we fail to realize our higher purpose as musicians. Does that make sense?"

"Yeah kind of," I replied. I said "kind of" because while I understood what he meant, for me art was very personal, and I didn't like being told what my motivation for making it should be. I was also miffed by the implication that by not playing for others I had somehow neglected a higher calling of some sort. I started feeling cagey and wanted to leave.

Heart Connections

He must have sensed my indifference because he motioned for me to let him sit at the piano and said, "Allow me to demonstrate." We then traded places and he proceeded to effortlessly play a passage of rich, swinging, jazzy, gospel music that filled me with good vibes and lifted my spirits.

But just as I was getting into it, he abruptly stopped playing, slouched his shoulders, turned his body away from mine so I couldn't see his face, and said in a melancholy tone, "Now listen to *this*..."

Then he played the *same* song, but very robotically and choppy, without *any* of the swinging rhythm, rich chord colors, dynamics, or expressiveness from his first performance. I couldn't believe my ears. It was the same song, but sounded lifeless and amateur, as though it were played by an entirely different musician. The contrast was remarkable.

Lifting his hands from the piano he deadpanned me and asked with smiling eyes, "Can you hear the difference between those two performances?"

"Yes of course."

"What was the difference you heard?" he asked.

"Well, for the first version you were at ease, and the music flowed with a lot of expression and passion, so it was really enjoyable. But in the second version.... well... not so much."

"Yes!" he exclaimed, pleased with my answer. "So is it fair to say the first version made a *connection* with you, but the second one didn't?"

"Yes, that's right," I acknowledged.

"OK, so here's the deal. Until you master the fundamentals and play for others a lot, you will not be able to play confidently from the heart and make a connection with people as I did with you. Does that make sense?"

I nodded in acknowledgment, but I didn't agree with his big idea that the purpose of music was to make connections with people. At the time I believed the purpose of music was artful expression. In fact, I frowned on those who consciously formulated their music to appeal to people.

Grimy Gift

Unfazed by my tepid response, he continued passionately. "You see, musical talent is a *gift*, and gifts are meant to be shared. So every time you pay it forward and share the gift, it becomes a valuable gift to someone else and completes the circle of giving. But if you don't invest the time to polish your gift, it won't be as valuable to people. Does that make sense?"

I nodded again because I didn't have the energy to argue, but I still wasn't tracking with him. I didn't consider music to be a "gift" and I didn't care if my music "moved people." In my view, music was art and nothing more.

He then grabbed the out-of-place green and red elf figurine from the cabinet shelf and handed it to me. "Here Mark, here's a *gift* from me to you. What do you think about it?"

I turned the figurine over in my hand and noticed it was grimy and caked with dust, as though it had never been cleaned. Smiling cordially, I said, "Thank you."

"Well? Do you like it?" he asked.

"It's a nice gesture," I said.

"Are you being honest?"

Sigh. "OK, in all honesty it doesn't look like you took great care of it so..."

"Ah! So you're saying you would value it more if I had taken better care of it before I gave it to you?"

"Yes, I guess I am," I conceded.

"Well, that's the same way listeners feel when musicians haven't invested the time to polish their gift."

"That's an interesting perspective," I said, handing the figurine back to him. I understood what he was saying, but admittedly I wasn't too enthusiastic about the whole "mastering the fundamentals" thing. Going back to basics and spending hours of my life doing robotic drills was beneath me to say the least.

Still unfazed by my resistance, he demonstrated a finger-strengthening exercise called "Hanons," and said they would serve as a great starting point for me to *master the fundamentals.* The fingering actually looked simple, so I assumed it would be easy when he asked me to try to play them. But nope. I hit so many wrong notes I couldn't even get past the first few chords. Humbled again.

Another Direction

After the lesson he walked me outside. As we stood next to my car, he embraced me in another bear hug and assured me that if I became his piano student, he would teach me to *play from the heart and make amazing connections with people.* He added, "Remember, all great masters were first great students."

I thanked him and asked how much money I owed for the lesson. He said the best way I could repay him was by "paying it forward and doing the same for someone else someday." Unaccustomed to that level of kindness from a stranger, I confess I found it hard to believe he didn't have an ulterior motive.

That night I felt a mix of emotions. On one hand, I was uplifted by his encouragement and felt like I made a great ally. I couldn't recall ever meeting someone who was so accepting and kind, who shared their knowledge so generously. He was like a beacon of light at a time when I was straining to see any light at all.

On the other hand, I was seeking a guide, not a regimented professor. At 40 years old I had no interest in being his or anyone else's "student." Moreover, I was in the throes of divorce, and all his preachy hubbub about "playing from the heart to connect with people" and "sharing gifts" was not only unappealing but rubbed me wrong and made me uncomfortable. I was all about "music for the *art*," not "music for the heart."

After deciding he wasn't a good fit for me, I sent him an email the next day saying, "Thanks for your time, but I've decided to go another direction." His reply was, "No problem at all, but I'm here for you anytime if you have any questions—or just want to talk! ((smile)). Keep persevering, master those fundamentals, and it will pay off!"

I thought that was the last I'd ever hear from him. God must have been laughing again.

Reflections

To my frustration, Mateo turned out to be the opposite of what I was seeking. But as much as I disagreed with his teachings, he treated me like a brother—or a son, I couldn't decide which—and I felt an inexplicable kinship with him. Had I not been so blinded with self-righteous pride, I might have seen his sage wisdom about *learning fundamentals* and *playing from the heart for others* applied to much more in life than mastering the piano.

Thankfully, by the grace of God, despite my puffed-up closed-mindedness, and unbeknownst to me, the learning seeds of truth had been sown.

9: Close Encounters

"Therefore... let each one of you speak the truth with his neighbor, for we are members one of another." -Ephesians 4:25 (NKJV)

Rebecca: Despite a few hiccups all was going well in my world when I was suddenly broadsided by a series of financial setbacks, job problems, and other issues. Unable to find immediate pain relief from praying and church, I started drinking and going out with friends frequently. At first it felt good, but then I had a really bad experience and the fun came to an abrupt end.

Divine Faith Formula

Then one morning my daughter was listening to worship music, and I heard a song about waiting patiently on God and obeying Him even when you're stressed and can't see the way forward. It brought back to mind all the lessons I learned at the retreat and moved me to pray again. I said, "Dear Heavenly Father, I lift up my heart to you. I need your strength and wisdom. I can't do this on my own. Show me the way because I can't see it."

That Sunday I was back at church with a renewed hunger for God's comfort and wisdom. God didn't disappoint. After the heart-warming worship songs, the sermon was about how we must remain in Christ and find strength from Him to resist temptations when faced with trials and hardships. I read along with the pastor as he spoke the words of Jesus aloud to the congregation:

"Remain in Me, and I also will remain in you. No branch can bear fruit by itself; it must remain in the vine. Neither can you bear fruit unless you remain in Me. I am the vine and you are the branches. If you remain in Me, and I in you, you will bear *much* fruit; apart from me you can do *nothing*." -John 15:4 (NIV)

I was saying "amen" and praising God with everyone else in the room as he read those words—until he explained what they meant.

"On a sunny day it's an easy formula to follow, right?" he asked the congregation. "But not so much when a difficult trial comes. Trials bring out painful emotions like sadness, fear, anxiety, and anger, and they result in suffering. And we all hate suffering, right?

"So we ask God to deliver us. But when He doesn't respond as fast as we want Him to, what happens? We disconnect from the vine and instead go out on a worldly limb like drugs, alcohol, partying, dangerous lifestyles, and what not to stop the pain. Then what happens? The limb always breaks doesn't it? Then we end up sick, weak, confused, and lost."

I couldn't disagree because I had done that very thing when God didn't get me out of pain as fast as I desired.

"But it doesn't have to be that way!" the pastor continued, as though he had heard my thought. "We can stay connected to Jesus and keep obeying His commands when faced with trial and suffering.

"The Bible has the answer in Psalms 27:13 (NKJV) 'Wait on the LORD; Be of good courage, And He shall strengthen your heart; Wait, I say, on the LORD!' That means perseverance. What is perseverance? Perseverance is a long *obedience* in the same direction.

"How can we keep obeying God during difficult trials? Same way Paul and the apostles did in The Book of Acts: With the *power* of the Holy Spirit. How do we get the power of the Holy Spirit? Instead of going to bad habits and bad people when we get hit with bad news or bad storms, we go to Jesus.

"How do we go to Jesus? We draw *close* to Him for truth, direction, rest, nourishment, and strength for our souls. We pray without cease. And we wait faithfully for God's perfect timing. That's the only way to real truth, understanding, and healing. Jesus is the great deliverer, and He will deliver us if we abide in Him and persevere in faith."

Once again it was as if the sermon had been written specifically for me by God Himself. It gave me the chills, it encouraged me, it inspired me, but most of all it humbled me to tears of gratitude. My faith had once again been strengthened that my heavenly Father was all wise and would provide for all my needs... if I could just learn to trust Him and be patient.

Heart to Heart

The next week I prayed daily for God's wisdom and strength to persevere through my trials with trust and patience. Miraculously by Friday I no longer had the desire to party. Instead I attended a women's retreat, where I spent time with Sarah and other ladies from the church.

At one point we broke off into groups and Sarah, who had become like a big sister to me, asked how I was doing. I shared how I was working through a lot of resentment and couldn't wait until my divorce was final so I could celebrate. Her reply leveled me.

"We've been praying for you," she said sweetly. "Praying that you have strong faith and follow the will of God, because only God knows what your heart truly needs to be happy, Rebecca."

"I've definitely been trying to follow His will, but it can be hard," I said, suddenly feeling emotional.

"I know you have, and I couldn't be prouder of you for your progress. So just know it's totally out of love when I say this to you. I know your marriage was hard, and that you feel you have to move on, but God doesn't celebrate divorce, and neither should we. Just remain humble, exercise faith, and wait for His will to be fully revealed."

I wasn't angry, but all of my defense mechanisms kicked in. I assured her our marriage was a train wreck, that Mark and I were on opposite ends of the universe, that I had lost all hope that we could ever have a happy marriage, and that I had moved on and would never go back. She listened intently, and I could tell by the look in her eyes that my words resonated with her.

I assumed she would say she was sorry (like most people did when they heard my sad marriage song) and that would be that. But I couldn't have been more wrong. She leaned forward, put her hand on mine, and said, "I feel your pain, and your pain is real, and I believe every word you said, but I need to share something with you that I've been holding back."

Fearing the worst, I braced for some sort of lecture. But instead she proceeded to pluck every string of my heart with her dramatic marriage testimony.

I was stunned to learn that her seemingly happy and harmonious marriage, the one whom young people and adults alike at the church looked upon as a role model for Christian marriage and stability, had faced giant obstacles earlier on and even shipwrecked at one point. She told me the issues were so severe that her marriage teetered on divorce at one point.

She testified it was only due to God's *grace*, after her and her husband mutually surrendered their lives to Christ, that they finally got on the same page and eventually were blessed with a strong foundation to build their marriage on. She also shared the many ways theirs hearts had been softened and how harmonious their marriage had become.

Her testimony was so brutally truthful, yet at the same time so passionate, humble of heart, and loving that I broke down in tears and hugged her. I had never heard anything so honest and reverent in my life. I realized the radiant love I often felt in her presence was the love of Christ in her servant heart.

Then suddenly I saw the difference between us. I had not been a devoted Christian woman of faith in my marriage like her. For the first time I wondered if my marriage would have been different if I had been different. I even felt a twinge of guilt for not being more sensitive and patient with Mark given all of his career stress.

But then I caught myself. *Who was I fooling?* Even if I were to have faith like Sarah, Mark would never open his heart and have faith. Mark wasn't humble enough to admit he needed God like Sarah's husband had. He was the last guy in the world who would ever turn his life over to Jesus.

So, despite Sarah's lovely testimony, I pushed it out of my mind and assured myself that whatever I was learning had nothing to do with Mark. I reasoned God was most likely strengthening my resolve to get out of my toxic marriage and stop looking back. I couldn't imagine there was any way God wanted me to return to a sunken ship marriage and break my back trying to resurrect it—especially when every fiber of my being said we would fail. *Never, ever, ever, EVER*, I vowed again.

A friend of mine outside the church reinforced my position a few days later. When I told her about Sarah's testimony she responded, "It sounds really nice in theory, and in perfect world yeah OK, but she doesn't know your whole story, or the stuff you have dealt with. If she did, she would be praying for your divorce!" I had to laugh because it was true—or so I thought.

But an unexpected thing happened after that: I couldn't get Sarah's testimony out of my mind. I couldn't stop thinking about how loving, patient, and perseverant she had been with her husband. Then came more conviction, followed by more guilt and an intensifying feeling that God was trying to tell me something.

Uninvited Prayer

A few days later while I was searching for an email in my inbox, I came across the email Mark sent previously. I read it a second time and was taken by his humility and the fact that he had actually listened to me for once. But then I caught myself again. "No!" I said out loud. For all I knew he had an ulterior motive, such as buttering me up so he could try to patch us back up again.

That night I attended youth group with our kids and chatted with one of the leaders named Mary, who also had an amazing marriage like Sarah. Somehow we started talking about love, and once again I found myself rehashing my irreconcilable marriage and explaining how toxic it was.

As we were about to leave for the evening, Mary pulled me aside and asked if she could pray with me. I was nervous because I had no idea what she wanted to pray about. But given how sweet she was I couldn't imagine it was anything weird, so I agreed.

We then went to a dark classroom, turned on the lights, and to my astonishment she grabbed my hands and proceeded to pray for my—*marriage! What?*

Then came words that I never dreamed I would hear. "Father in heaven, we come to you this evening in humble prayer to ask that you reconcile the marriage of Rebecca and her husband...."

Whoa! I wasn't expecting that. I was even more surprised when she started crying, which touched me so deeply that I started crying too, even though a reconciliation with Mark was the last thing in the world I wanted. I was back in the Twilight Zone again.

When she finished her prayer, we hugged, and I thanked her. Then I gently told her I had lost hope that our marriage could be saved but appreciated her sentiment. Her response was strikingly similar to Sarah's. "There's always hope if you have faith, so just trust God, and He will reveal His will."

All I could do was smile and nod because I was at a complete loss.

After the youth group my plan was to go out with my friends since the kids were staying at my brother's house. But on the way home I suddenly recalled times in our marriage when I had not been responsible, or forced my will on Mark, or had been ungrateful. And then I felt deeply convicted and wrong for planning a divorce party.

The conviction was so powerful that it moved me to apologize to God out loud. As I prayed, I was overcome by contrition and moved to apologize to Mark also. Suddenly it hit me that I needed to stop fighting and wave the flag of surrender... so I could be at peace with God, and so Mark and I could move on in peace.

So, I grabbed a white napkin out of my center console and began writing. Then I drove to Marks' house, took a deep breath, and knocked on his door.

Reflections

Notice I said I turned to drinking and partying after I couldn't find any "immediate" relief from prayer and church. That's a testament to what I would later learn was a lifelong pattern of impatience and demand for immediate results (or, in Biblical words, lack of self-control). Fortunately, God pulled me off the limb I had gone out on before it broke and brought me back into the presence, *presence*, of His truth and wise counselors again

The pastor's point about the desire to be released from painful emotions and suffering really struck home. It hit me that I had always acted on my emotions—rather than praying and waiting patiently for the Lord's response. I would learn eventually it was a character defect that impacted my relationships greatly. The sermon made me realize how impatient I was, and how much I needed God to overcome it.

But as powerful as the sermon was, Sarah's unexpected testimony (and Mary's prayer) was even more powerful. Through her testimony the Holy Spirit had softened my heart and moved me to repentance and forgiveness. And that was (in hindsight) a total miracle I never thought possible. I had been convinced I was the victim of a bad marriage and had done nothing wrong. God now seemed to be convincing me otherwise... and I wasn't fighting Him... yet.

The *Last* Breakup

10: Closing Arguments

"For nothing is secret that will not be revealed, nor anything hidden that will not be known and come to light." -Luke 8:17 (NKJV)

Mark: Despite my "thanks, but no thanks" email to Mateo, he continued to send invitations to meet again as well as encouraging notes of all kinds. Though I was annoyed, it was hard to be mad at him when his messages said things like, "Mark, you are very gifted and talented, and I know you'll be <u>playing from the heart</u> like a pro if you stay <u>committed</u> to learning and applying the <u>fundamentals</u> (((smile)))."

At some point his perseverance wore me down and I secretly began practicing the "Hanon" exercises. In full disclosure my instant-gratification-oriented-self hated the exercises with a passion. They tried my patience like nothing I had ever encountered (including meditation). It was all I could do to laboriously clang my way through all the keys without screaming. And that's what I was doing one evening when I heard a knock on the front door.

Owning It

When I opened the door, I was startled to find Rebecca standing in front of me with a conciliatory expression on her face and a folded napkin in her hand. I was even more startled when she asked if we could sit down and talk. I had no idea what she was thinking and braced for impact as I led her through the house to the backyard patio.

Sitting across from each other, she cleared her throat and solemnly said words I never fathomed I would hear. "So... going to church, learning God's word and being surrounded by faithful Christian people has taught me a lot about myself and mistakes I've made," she said, holding back tears. "I've learned that I fell short of being the best wife, mom, and friend I could be. So I would like to apologize for the following...."

She then unfolded the napkin and to my utter shock read a list of things she wished she had done better: from taking more of an interest in my passions, to being more empathetic about my work challenges, to acting more responsibly, to being more patient, sensitive, and so forth.

She concluded by saying her goal was to be a good Christian woman, that she wouldn't be throwing a divorce party, and how she hoped we could be friends, especially for the kids' sake.

Beyond my utter shock, my skin shivered with goosebumps and my heart exalted in chilling waves of gratitude, relief, and joy. Not only was it the first time she took responsibility for her part in our collapse, it was the first time she sincerely apologized to me since I had known her. It was a miracle.

Exhilarated by her merciful, soul-stirring confession and apparent metamorphosis, I reflexively jumped up and hugged her tightly. As we embraced, I sensed a tiny spark of what felt like love between us for the first time in a long while.

Thinking she must have read my apology email, I blurted, "Wow! So... did you get my email?"

"Yes," she said as she wiped tears from her face, "but I've been going to church and hearing a lot of testimonies... and God has been revealing a lot of truth about my mistakes... and I realized I need to own them and stop blaming you and others. I want us both to heal and hopefully be friends."

She was like a completely new person. Her humble confession was so powerful it compelled me to apologize for not being a caring and accepting friend, not making our relationship a priority, and most of all, taking her for granted. She thanked me and reiterated how much she hoped we could be friends. Then I lost it.

Boiling Point

Suddenly my heart melted, and I felt such deep gratitude and love for her that I was moved to put my hand on hers and gush, "So what if we started our marriage over, this time as friends first?" I couldn't believe my own words.

Boom! Confession session over. She ripped her hand from mine, jumped to her feet, and backed away like I was a dangerous animal. "STOP! Don't do that," she commanded.

And just like *that*, every inch of lost ground I thought we had made up was gone, and the gulf between us was once again wider and deeper than the Grand Canyon. "Buuut... I thought... since we apologized and all..." I stammered.

"It's not about apologizing," she overruled me. "It's about giving your whole heart to your marriage, which you've never wanted to do, and never will, because it's just... not who you are."

"Wait, what do you mean by not giving my *whole heart*?" I asked forlornly.

"You know what I mean."

"No, I don't," I insisted, feeling my blood pressure rising. "I've sacrificed for you since day *one*. That's why I agreed to kids, gave up my musical dreams, and took a corporate grind job."

"*You've* sacrificed?" she laughed bitterly, "I delivered two babies and gave my whole life for our family while you spent all your free time doing things that made *you* happy. Please don't talk to me about sacrifice."

"That's ridiculous!" I contended. "I've always done stuff for you and the kids, I've—"

"Are you joking? Marriage and family have never been your passions."

"Wait a minute, where does it say marriage and family are supposed to be my *passions*? That's not even realistic, that's—"

"It's not realistic for *you,*" she countered. "It's totally realistic for other men, just not for *you,* because you only think of your own happiness. I've met Christian men who *love* being best friends with their wives, and they are happy, and—"

"*Best friends? Puhleeeeze!*" I mocked. "Those guys are frauds. They put on a show for the world, but behind closed doors they're miserable. Trust me, true happiness only comes from hard work and accomplishment, which is called self-actualization."

"News flash Mark, I know this may come as a shock, but not everyone thinks like you. Believe it or not, a lot of people do find happiness from being in God's love and sharing their time and lives with others, not self-actuality, or whatever you call it."

"Time? I spent loads of time with you," I said. But no matter how much time I gave, it was never enough."

"You only spent time with me when it made *you* happy! You gave all your time to your dreams, not me."

"That's not true!" I yelled. It was everything I could do to refrain from lashing out in an expletive-laced defense. But I felt an impulse to calm down, and after deep-breathing a few times I miraculously regained my composure.

Then, as she pulled open the sliding door to leave, she said, "I apologized for my part because I was hoping for closure, not to try to patch us up again. You need to let go. You don't want me and never did. Let go. We are over."

Her words were like daggers being thrust into my heart and made me physically sick to my stomach, *"Let go? What are you talking about? You're falsely accusing me."*

Tail lights

Back inside the house I clenched my teeth and took deep breaths to stay calm as we made our way to the front door. I tried to convince myself she was so hypocritically lost that it was pointless to say anything else. But my attempt at self-control was no match for my indignation.

As she walked down the driveway I said, "Don't insult God and say you want to be a better Christian when you are adamant about divorce that will tear our family apart." *Incoming...*

She spun around and said, "Family? More like a *pretend* family. We put on a good show on the outside, but on the inside, we lived separate lives in separate rooms. I'm pretty sure God would rather we found some happiness than continue to *pretend* we have a happy life."

"*Happiness?* Sorry but you're being misled," I tried to school her. "There are no shortcuts to happiness, and no marriage or family is perfect. Happiness comes from sticking to your commitments, like my mom and dad have stuck with their marriage for 45 years."

"Sorry but I'm not staying in a marriage with someone who clearly doesn't like being married so I can say I *stuck it out*," she argued. "I'm sick of pretending. A Christian marriage is not supposed to be ball and chain misery, it's supposed to be a friendship, filled with togetherness and love of God and—"

"Yeah right!" I howled. "No one has that kind of marriage! I can't believe you've bought into those televangelist lies. Science proves men and women are not even compatible to begin with. Marriage is work, not a joy ride."

At that she smiled and nodded, as if I had confirmed something she knew to be true all along, and said, "You're right. We're not compatible and never have been. Now can you PLEASE let go so everyone can move on?"

Before I could answer, she turned and walked briskly toward her car. I yelled after her, "And stop taking our kids to that church."

"No," she said firmly as she got into her car. "they love our church, and I'm not taking them out. Bye!"

I was so angry at myself for opening up my heart and getting trampled I couldn't think straight. But as I watched her tail lights disappear into the night, my fury was temporarily overshadowed by a profound sense of loss unlike any I felt from our previous separations.

Then again, in the past I had always been able to convince her to try again. Evidently my "let's-patch-things-up" persuasive power was gone. Evidently she wasn't buying it anymore.

Rebecca: After Mark tried to patch us up again and set off all my protective defenses, I tried my best to refrain from telling him all the ugly truths about his selfishness that I had been realizing. I had no desire to hurt him even further or give him the idea I was trying to resolve our marriage. But when he belittled me and acted like his way was the only way, and implied I was being brainwashed, I lost it.

Losing It

Mark: That night I took my anger and sorrow to the phone to vent-rant to friends again. Once again everyone validated me—except my friend Alyssa. After she heard my newest rant, she threw another unsettling curve ball. "I'm concerned you're losing it, and I really think you should see a grief counselor, friend."

Losing it? Grief counselor?? I was appalled she was treating me like some sort of pitiful co-dependent. "No. I don't need some overeducated, overpaid *counselor*," I shot back. "I can fix my own problems. I'm just blowing off some stream," I assured her.

But the next day when I was sober, I realized she was right again—at least about the "losing it" part. Regardless of whether or not Rebecca's accusations were true, they were devastating, and my alcohol-fueled rants were only multiplying the agony and making me look like a blustering fool to my friends.

I finally conceded I was a mess of conflicted emotions and confusion and needed some sort of help. I decided it was time for new therapy—of the High Sierra mountain kind. *If anything could get mind off the drama and reclaim my life,* I reasoned, *it was a return to my roots, and some time with people who loved me unconditionally.*

The next day I packed my suitcase and prepared to depart for Lake Tahoe, CA, to visit my parents for a Labor Day Weekend retreat. I intended to take my problems to the top of the mountain and leave them there. That was my intent anyway.

Reflections

Mark: Shockingly, Rebecca's soul-stirring peace offering led to fresh round of blistering accusations that sent me into another emotional tailspin. I was appalled that she attacked my character and integrity (again) and degraded my long-held beliefs and values. I was incensed that she was hypocritically preaching to me about God and love out of one side of her mouth, while vowing to never return to our marriage out of the other. And I was frustrated to the point of exasperation that her views about everything (including me) were rapidly and radically changing... and there was absolutely nothing I could do about it.

Rebecca: I came to make peace but was drawn back into war when Mark tried to patch us up again. I actually wasn't even consciously aware of how much resentment I had towards Mark, or even how much my beliefs had changed, until I was backed into a corner and forced to defend myself.

Ironically, Mark accused me of doing a bait and switch, but that's what *he* did. Previously, he said he wanted to be friends, so I took a leap of faith and honestly shared my heart to make peace; but instead of listening and respecting me, I thought he tried to leverage my vulnerability to patch us up again.

It was a painful reminder why I didn't trust him (or anyone else) with my heart. All that said, I still had a lot to learn.

Mark: Speaking retrospectively, beyond all of our impassioned emotions and regret for meeting, our bi-polar blowout wasn't the loss either of us thought it was at the time. Unbeknownst to us, by the grace of God, we had both honestly submitted to various degrees, and the truth had finally, after 14 years of being locked up, begun to break free. That said, I still had a lot more to learn than Rebecca, and I would have to go into the depths of the wilderness to find it...

The *Last* Breakup

11: Disillusion Wilderness

"When I surveyed all that my hands had done and what I had toiled to achieve, everything was meaningless, a chasing after the wind; nothing was gained under the sun."
-Ecclesiastes 2:11 (NIV)

Mark: After the patio blowout with Rebecca, I hoped a little time in the mountains on "higher ground" could lift my spirits and bring about some much-needed peace. But as I steered my way up the mountain road to my childhood home, I felt that deep sense of hopelessness return, and wondered if my demons had come along for the ride. *Hello darkness my familiar friend,* I groaned. Then came the dreadful idea that I was just spinning my wheels again—figuratively and literally.

Burned

After a happy homecoming day with my parents, I went to bed early and hoped to get a solid night's rest. But as soon as my head hit the pillow Rebecca's accusations and delusional ideas about happiness came flooding back into my mind with a vengeance and wouldn't let me sleep. So much for peace.

Fortunately, the next morning brought good news when my dad invited me to take a mountain hike. Relishing the chance for some rare father-son bonding, I didn't hesitate to say yes. Long story short: due to my teenage transgressions and his stonewalling, we never really bonded and had an unsettled relationship at best. I was elated to finally spend some "guy time" with him.

Later that afternoon we were trekking through the woods to Desolation Wilderness. "Desolation," as my dad called it, was a heavily-forested mountain range where he often hiked and knew the terrain like the back of his hand.

As we made our way up the mountain, I asked him where we were going. He said, "Well, I figure we can get over to Tahoe Mountain and back home before it gets dark. Have to be mindful of the time. Don't want to make that mistake again."

"What mistake is that?" I asked.

"Well, I often hike to fishing holes deep in the wilderness, so I always plan carefully to make sure there is enough daylight to get back to my car. One time I became so focused on catching a fish that I lost track of time. Looked at my watch and about died when I realized the sun was about to set in 30 minutes. Heh."

"What was the problem?" I asked.

"The problem was that the hike back to civilization was an hour and a half."

"*Oh wow!* Don't tell me you had to hike down the mountain in the dark?"

"Yep," he answered, with the pride of a conquering explorer. "Never been so scared in my life. There was no moon that night, and I didn't know if I would be eaten by a mountain lion or end up at the bottom of a cliff."

"Wow!" I said, feeling chills as I pictured myself facing the same dilemma. "But obviously you made it."

"Yep. The last half hour was the killer. I was literally *feeling* my way out of there at times. My only saving grace was a tiny light in the distance. I just kept walking towards that light. Funny, I left rock piles to find my way back, but none of them were any help when it was pitch black. I took a few bad tumbles. Hard to believe it wasn't worse."

"That's awful!" I said.

"Yeah. Speaking of awful, wait until you see this," he said, pointing ahead of him.

When I reached his side and realized what he was pointing to, my jaw fell open. Instead of seeing the familiar lush green and slate landscape of countless childhood adventures, all I saw were hundreds of acres of charcoaled, scorched, fire-ravaged earth. "Good Lord!" I gasped, feeling sick.

We were looking at the ugly aftermath of a major fire that had come within a mile and a half of my parents' home a few months earlier. Nauseous from the sight of it, I was hesitant to proceed. But he wanted to continue on, so I nervously followed.

Soon we were in the eye of what had been a raging inferno only a few months before, our spirits dampened, our voices mournfully silent. Save for the distant squawk of a lone Blue Jay, the only sound was the rhythmic crunch of charcoaled timber under our ash-coated hiking boots. *Crunch, crunch, crunch.* It was like walking through a war zone.

With the acrid smell of nature's demise in my nose and its blackened devastation filling my eyes, I marveled at how a tiny ember could explode into such a ruthless wrecking machine. In a microcosmic sense it reminded me of my failed marriage (if not my whole life): how it started with a spark but raged into a firestorm that burned a trail of damage in its wake.

I recalled once reading, "A fire can either warm or burn you, it all depends on where you stand." I shook my head sorrowfully because when it came to the fire of love, 40 years into life I still hadn't figured out where to stand.

Is That All There Is?

Eventually we arrived at the other side of the scorched ruins. I never thought I'd be so happy to see plain old, undefiled dirt. A few minutes later we were ascending above the valley of darkness. I marveled at the beauty all around and remarked, "Wow I forgot how beautiful it is up here. "

"Yep," my dad replied. "Mother Nature always teaches something new. John Muir [the naturalist] said, 'in every walk with nature, one receives far more than he seeks,' and I have found that to be accurate."

"Sounds good to me. This divorce drama has sucked the life out of me, so I'll take all the help I can get."

"Well, I'm sorry you're going through that," he said warmly. His sympathy always cheered me up.

"The worst part is she's been trying to make me feel guilty..." I said between labored breaths. "She's going to church now... telling me we had a *pretend* marriage... that there's more to marriage than sticking it out... that *real* happiness only comes from following God and love, and not self-actualizing. Isn't that ridiculous??"

I was certain he would agree with me, but to my shock he sighed heavily and replied with a question that would change everything.

"Well, I'm the wrong guy to ask about happiness, because I've lived a long time, and I've been down every road, and I can't help but wonder: *is that all there is?"*

Whoa. I wasn't sure I heard him right. "What do you mean?"

"Just what I told you. Is that all there is? What's the point?"

"What's the point of what? Of *life??"*

"Of *everything*," he concluded, as if he didn't want to talk about it any further.

I couldn't believe my ears. I had *just* lectured Rebecca on how life was all about hard work, and that fulfilling happiness only came later when you could stand tall atop the mountain of your accomplishment and declare *VICTORY!* I had even cited my dad as an example.

Yet here he was atop the mountain, with a plethora of accomplishments under his belt— including a 45-year marriage—and he wasn't declaring victory at all; he was declaring something more like defeat.

According to my self-realization philosophy he should be beaming with joy from his accomplishments... yet shockingly he seemed unhappier than I was... and I was divorcing!

My mind raced with questions. *What could possibly be missing from his life?* He believed in God (I think?), was in great health, had an amazing mind, a 45-year marriage, a beautiful and loving wife, three loving kids, gorgeous surroundings, endless talents, passions, knowledge, and personal milestones. I couldn't wrap my mind around it.

He personified the "American Dream"! I mean, if he was the "wrong" guy to ask about happiness, who was the "right" guy to ask? He had everything! Or did he? Maybe there was something else he had yet to find? But what could it be? I was totally mystified.

For some reason we didn't speak much as we hiked our way up to the summit. When we finally got to the top, his disillusioning question was still hanging over me like a dark cloud, and the Sierra sights didn't appear as majestic as I hoped they would. After spending a few minutes atop the precipice, we hit the trail again and made our way home.

Just as the sun was about to set, we were back in the valley of death, sulking across its ashen floor, my heart aching for both of our disillusioned souls. It struck me we were like sons of the wilderness, in search of something that might not even exist. Then I had the appalling, nihilistic thought that perhaps there was no point to life after all.

Then came the inner voice of defeat again saying, *Face it, life is nothing but one big, giant game played for the pleasure of a few, and you're just a pawn in it. Every man is just like a tree in the forest: he lives, the fire comes and engulfs him one day, and he dies. And if there is a God, He left this planet a long time ago.*

Thankfully my morbid lamentation was suddenly interrupted when my eyes were drawn to something extraordinary on the ground. It was a lone flower that had bloomed after the fire, and it was poking out defiantly from the ashes of death in radiant lavender splendor as if to say, "Behold, life!"

It seemed like a divine reminder that even from the darkest valley of death new life finds a way. It restored my hope for the moment, and I wondered if God was answering my nihilistic question, saying, "Son, if beauty and life are still here, I am still here."

Wrestling

That night, wrestling with endless new questions (or perhaps demons) about life, love, marriage, happiness, and more I didn't sleep well again. The next day I felt so burned out and deflated I decided to drive home a day early. It was sad to say goodbye to my parents, but I was too lost in thought to be socially functional.

Descending into the hot, smoggy valley I felt the crushing weight of all my anguish and disillusionment bearing down on me like a 300-pound barbell. I couldn't believe my latest attempt to find some validation and peace so I could move on from Rebecca was another utter failure.

Not only that, but my dad's existential question undermined the self-fulfillment foundation I had literally pillared all my hopes and dreams on (the same one Rebecca had flippantly dismissed) and left me to wonder who I was and what I stood for.

In the face of such existential angst and the absence of any kind of consolation, I questioned God and demanded answers again. "Why is everything I've ever put my hope in crumbling? Why am I facing all these questions? Why can't I just move on like everyone else? What have I done to deserve this?"

As I made the final descent into the valley, it hit me the divorce had been worse than the marriage. What started out as a quest for peace had somehow turned into a series of misfortunes, losses, and now an existential war in my soul. I was lost, deflated, and hopeless. I had the thought that one more defeat might very well break me. Talk about a prophecy.

I've heard it's always darkest before dawn. I'm a witness.

Reflections

I went to the mountain hoping to find some peace and validation. Not only did I fail to find them, but learning my dad's personal accomplishments hadn't led him to fulfilling happiness left me to wonder if I had been searching my whole life for a treasure that didn't exist.

If that was true, I didn't know which was the more painful truth: that I had lived my whole life postponing joy for future fulfillment that was never going to come, or that Rebecca's new beliefs about God and love were right and I was wrong. Both outcomes were unconscionable.

Sensing an intensifying fear that everything I ever stood on was shifting and sliding under my feet, I felt an urgent need to start digging in new places for answers, because all of my existing knowledge wells had suddenly run dry.

12: Labor Day Revelations

"Call to me and I will answer you and tell you great and unsearchable things you do not know." -Jeremiah 33:3 (NIV)

"As water reflects the face, so one's life reflects the heart." -Proverbs 27:19 (NIV)

Mark: It was around noon when I got back from my Tahoe trip. Driving down the last street leading to my neighborhood, I hit every red light, and it made me think of how many proverbial red lights I had hit on the road to divorce so far. As I approached the last intersection, the light was yellow, but of course I arrived seconds too late and was forced to stop and wait.

Boats Out of Water

Then it happened. As I sat waiting at the intersection for the light to change, I was shocked to see an SUV towing a waterski boat pass in front of my eyes... and in it was Rebecca, our kids and people I'd never seen before... laughing and having a great time.

Oof. Ffffwhat?! I couldn't believe my eyes. I couldn't believe the improbable timing. What were the chances I'd be sitting right there at that very second when they passed in front of me? But more than that, why were they so happy? Then of course I thought the worse: *It's her divorce party!!*

HONK HONK! I was so lost in thought I didn't realize the light had turned green, and the car behind me wasn't happy I hadn't noticed.

Back home as I unpacked, I tried to assure myself that everything happens for a reason. *Maybe I was there at that second so I could see Rebecca had moved on and finally get closure,* I reasoned. *Maybe she isn't as happy as she appears, but just trying to make the best of it.*

Unfortunately, my consolations failed, and soon all I wanted to do was sleep to make the pain go away. But just as I closed my eyes, I was aroused by the sound of playful laughter outside. I would have ignored it, but it sounded eerily like my own son and daughter, so I walked to the front room to investigate. When I peeked through the window blinds to the street outside, I couldn't believe my eyes.

Directly in front of my house was a boat exactly like the one Rebecca's SUV had been towing. My mind raced with questions. *What in the world? What is she doing here? What*—but then I realized it wasn't her. It was my next-door neighbor Matt and his wife and kids. They were loading recreational toys and supplies into their boat for a family outing.

Oof. It was painful to see such a loving, happy family portrait in my own front yard right after seeing my own my own divided family sailing down the road without me at the intersection. *There must be a reason,* I thought. *There's always a reason for everything....*

Man in the Mirror

I was just about to turn away from the window when my eyes were drawn to Matt. As he hustled back and forth between his garage and the boat, endearingly interacting with his wife and kids, it occurred to me how engaged, content, even *passionate* he was. Just as the man I had seen with the woman and the baby stroller, it appeared as though he would rather be nowhere else. *Whoa.*

Then I felt a powerful jolt from somewhere deep in my inner being and suddenly knew why I was standing there looking out my window: GOD was showing me a man who "played from his heart for others." A man who was passionate about marriage and family and "treated his wife like gold." A real man who was giving his *whole heart* for the good of others.

But before I could grasp the enormity of that revelation, my eyes were suddenly drawn from the scene outside to the reflection in the window. And there I saw my own face. And upon seeing my face I suddenly became aware of how different the man outside the window was in contrast to the one in its reflection. And in that instant, I realized what had been missing from our marriage. What had been missing was *me.*

My passion. My time. My whole heart and whole love. *Me.* I was missing from our marriage.

CRASH! That was the sound of my entire understanding of our marriage (including who was to blame for its failure), being shattered beyond recognition. At that instant I realized my heart was turned inward, jaded, and self-concerned... and that everything Rebecca said about me was... true.

No wonder! No wonder she was so determined to never reconcile. No wonder she was so impressed by the devoted husbands at her church. No wonder she was happily sailing down the road without me. Suddenly I understood her, empathized with her, and could no longer find it anywhere in my heart to be angry with her.

Then my concentration was abruptly broken by the sound of an engine starting. It was Matt and his family departing for their family outing.

The end.

I sullenly turned from the window and walked towards the living room. When I got there, I crashed on the sofa. I cried tears of relief because I could finally see what I thought was the reason for our marriage woes. I cried tears of regret because it had taken me so long to see it.

I spent the rest of the day replaying painful scenes from my life and marriage and marveling at my self-absorption and lack of self-awareness. And while there was no doubt in my mind I had experienced a divine revelation, I was deeply confused because I had no idea *why...* or if God would ever tell me.

Torn between gratitude for having learned the truth about my self-concerned heart, and grief that I would never get another chance to share it with Rebecca, I felt like I had received the winning lotto ticket but shown up to the lotto office a day too late to redeem it.

I was glad when the night came so I could escape the new storm of questions and thoughts that were pouring into my mind like water through the hole of a broken levee.

But my Labor Day pains weren't over yet...

Wilderness Revelation

Just before midnight I was jolted awake by a disturbing dream and couldn't get back to sleep. Figuring I might get sleepy if I read for a while, I headed to the front room to get a book. That's when my eyes were drawn to the red Bible on my end table... and I felt an irresistible urge to open it.

Despite childhood churching and strong religious beliefs, I had never actually opened a Bible before (other than to admire its density), so I had no idea where I should begin. I decided to flip through the pages and 'randomly' pick one. I landed on the Book of Jeremiah, on a page titled "Sin and Punishment." Then came the hurt...

"...they do not repent of their wickedness... each pursues their *own course* like a horse charging into battle... the wise are put to shame... behold they have rejected the word of the LORD... therefore I will give their wives to others, their fields to new owners; because from the least even to the greatest, everyone is greedy for gain... peace, peace, they say, when there is no peace..." -Jeremiah 8:6 (NIV)

There are no words to describe how shocked, disturbed, and convicted I felt as I read that passage. It was like a reading of my actual life. I had been shamed, my wife was gone, I had been greedy, and I had searched for peace but failed to find any. I was guilty as charged on every count, and just as God said, peace was far from me.

Hoping I had taken the Scripture out of context, I flipped through several chapters and stopped on another one. It was even more upsetting than the first:

"Cursed is the man who trusts in man and makes flesh his strength, whose heart departs from the LORD. For he... shall not see when good comes but shall inhabit the parched places in the wilderness... [but] blessed is the man who trusts in the LORD, and whose hope is the LORD whose confidence is in him. He will be like a tree planted by the water that sends out its roots by the stream. It does not fear when heat comes; its leaves are always green. It has no worries in a year of drought and never fails to bear fruit." -Jeremiah 17:5 (NIV)

Cursed! My whole life flashed before my eyes as it sank in that *I* was the man in the verse. I was the man whose *heart* had departed from God. I was the man who had been ungrateful and put all my confidence and hope in myself and the world instead of God. I was the man with shallow roots, dried out, burned up, hard of heart, and lost in the *wilderness.*

Then I remembered my dad's story about losing track of time in the wilderness and how he had to stumble out in the dark with nothing but a faint light in the distance to navigate by because it was too dark to see the navigational rock piles he made. I was that man too: while I was busy chasing my ambitions, the dark had fallen, my rock piles of worldly wisdom were of no use, and I was now stumbling in the dark—with no light to navigate by.

Feeling like I had just been proverbially convicted of treason and sentenced to life without parole in the wilderness, I finally closed the Bible, placed it on the end table, and sat down on the floor. Then I was moved to pray solemnly with only the tiniest sliver of faith:

"I'm so sorry God. Forgive me for wronging you and taking my blessings for granted. I didn't know what I was doing. I still don't know what I'm doing. Please have mercy on me. Show me a way out of this wilderness, teach me your way, and give me a chance to atone for my sins and redeem myself."

Wiping tears from my eyes I returned to bed. As I drifted off into what would be one of the deepest sleeps of my life, I didn't know if God had been humbling me to create something new and beautiful from the ashes of my life, or to bury me under a mountain of regret so high that I could never find my way out. I prayed it wasn't the latter.

Reflections

Shortly after we filed for divorce a friend told me the divorce process was full of painful surprises that would try my soul. At the time I laughed and assured him I was a warrior who could handle whatever life threw at me. After seeing Rebecca and my family sailing down the road without me I wasn't laughing anymore. My soul was thoroughly tried... and humbled down to what was left of its foundation. And I believe God had a reason for allowing it.

At the end of the previous chapter you might recall I "had the thought that one more defeat might very well break me." I'm thoroughly convinced God brought me to that intersection at that moment in time to break me... as in break the last bit of pride that was still blocking me from seeing the truth.

What truth? First the painful truth that my heart had been separated from my wife. Second, and more importantly, the jarring truth that my heart had been separated from God. The only problem was, I didn't understand the relationship between those two things yet... or how to fix them.

I was also convinced it had to be God that led me to the front window to see the vision of a man giving his whole heart for the good of others, as well as to my red Bible to read the convicting passages about being divided from God. I was convinced due to all the miraculously improbable events, as well as a spiritual, tacit-level knowledge that illuminated my heart and mind in a way that mere words cannot explain.

Looking back, I marvel at how fearful I was of God's wrath after reading Jeremiah. Due to my Biblical ignorance (and pride) I couldn't yet see God wasn't blasting me with truth to lock me in the basement with my demons for the rest of my life. I had been in a [self-imposed] "prison" for a long time. He was trying to break me out. I also couldn't yet see my true "deliverer."

And on that note, I didn't understand yet that I couldn't "atone and redeem myself," no matter how passionately I prayed to God. Nor could I see that while my heart had been missing from my marriage in many ways, it wasn't the missing link to our relationship, nor was anything else of this world.

13: Wakeup Calls

"The LORD is close to the broken-hearted and saves those who are crushed in spirit." -Psalm 34:18 (NIV)

Mark: The next morning after my painful Labor Day revelations and impassioned prayer to God, I woke to a miracle. To my complete astonishment most of the fear and anguish I had been feeling the night before was gone, and in its place was a new hope that God was giving me, the shattered man in the mirror, a chance to do right by Him and redeem myself.

Convinced I had undergone a miraculous change of heart and found the missing piece of our marriage puzzle, I decided I needed to call Rebecca right way and tell her about my revelations. I would witness the miracles. I would humbly apologize and ask her forgiveness. I would soften her heart and convince her to come back. I had it all planned out and began rehearsing what I would say. Me and my big plans.

Battling

But before I could call her, I received an unexpected call from my minister friend Aaron. *Strange timing again,* I thought. I was so eager to share my miraculous revelations and change of heart with someone I didn't hesitate to pick up.

"I've seen the light," I proudly declared.

"Oh really?" he laughed.

"Yep, I had a maaaajor epiphany and realized I had been putting my own ambitions first, and that's how the marriage fell apart. You were right: God was trying to get my attention, and it was to help me see the truth about why our marriage failed so I could make things right. My heart has been changed."

"Wow man, that's amazing!" he said. "You're seeking and finding, just like God promised. Keep seeking and you'll keep finding. God has so much more to share with you."

I glossed right over his preachy editorial. "Yeah, the only thing is, Rebecca has not been receptive to reconciling, so I'm trying to figure out how I should approach her."

"Hmm," he said. "Well, if she hasn't been receptive then that door might be closed right now. I wonder if you should ask God what He wants you to do and await His reply."

"Not an option," I asserted firmly, like a captain strategizing a battle plan. "Our divorce is set to finalize soon, so I don't have time for all that. Anyway, God only helps those who help themselves, right? It's not like He's going to fight my battles for me. I need to move quick before it's too late."

"Actually, God *will* fight your battles for you if you *let* Him," he corrected me. "The Bible says, 'with us is the Lord our God to help us, and to fight our battles.' We just have to give Him control and allow Him to fight for us. That's where faith comes in. So just leave your prayer on

God's doorstep and resist the temptation to keep going back to see if He got it." -2 Chronicles 32:7 (NIV)

God fights people's battles for them? That was news to me. I had always fought my own battles and didn't know any other way to fight. I was also pretty sure God had more important things to do than sort out my stupid marriage drama. I decided Aaron didn't know what he was talking about and forged ahead with my plan... like a horse charging into battle.

Nine to Zero

After rehearsing a few times, I dialed Rebecca's number and prayed for the best. "Come on God, one more chance," I prayed, as if I had just spun a roulette wheel.

"You won't believe what happened!" I said jubilantly when she answered.

"Mark, please—" she groaned.

I spoke rapidly. "Give me one minute, that's all I ask. So I was sitting at the intersection and saw you with your friends pulling a boat and it really hurt... but then I went home and witnessed the most amazing sight outside my window—"

"Wait. How—were you following me? Wait. Why are you doing this?" she demanded.

"Just hear me out," I pleaded, speaking even more rapidly. "When I looked out my window, I saw my neighbor Matt and his wife and kids... you know, a perfect little family like you always wanted... and it hit me like a ton of bricks that Matt was the kind of devoted husband and real man you told me about.

"Then *BOOM*, I figured out what was missing from our marriage all those years. It was *me!* I didn't give you my whole heart because I didn't have a whole heart to give. My heart was divided and hardened by pride. But I'm ready to change and start living for God and love."

Silence.

"Are you there? Did you hear me?" I asked.

"Yes, I heard you," she answered impatiently.

"You have to believe me. I've seen the light, and I know what you mean about not giving my whole heart to our marriage now. I didn't make time for love. I didn't make you my priority. I get it now."

Silence.

"Hello??"

"Ahem, yes, I'm here," she sighed.

"Well?"

"Look, I'm glad you get it," she finally relented. "I'm glad you finally see I wasn't being unreasonable over the years. You made me feel like I was crazy, and it hurt. But just admitting you were wrong doesn't *change* anything. You have to actually *change*. And even if you did... it's just too late. Our marriage is *over*. I've moved on. I'd never try again under any circumstances. Sometimes it's just too late. I have to go now."

I lost it. "But where's your... your... INTEGRITY? What happened to going to church and wanting to be a good Christian woman?"

"*Integrity??* Oh, let's not go there—" she halted mid-sentence and took a reset breath. "Mark, why in the world do you want to be with me? Aren't you tired of the pain?"

"Because I realize how much of your heart you've given to our marriage and family, and that you're the best thing that ever happened to me, the best friend I've ever had," I said, holding back tears.

I prayed she would hear my sincerity because I was speaking right from my open heart. But nope. She fired back with six of the most incendiary words I've ever heard:

"Jesus should be your best friend."

What?! I was beside myself. But before I could say anything she added, "And what do you care about *love*? You said love doesn't lead to happiness. So go live your self-reality thing—or whatever you call it—and find your happiness. But *please* leave me out of it!"

I wanted to tell her I had come to see God and love were the way of happiness, but she hung up before I had the chance. And just like *that*, my hope to redeem myself was gone, and I was right back in the wilderness again with no light to find my way out.

Hope Fading

Hoping to find some sort of consolation, I called my friend Alyssa and shared the latest episode with her. "It's just so wrong," I complained. "I never learned how to be a great husband, but now I've seen the light and my heart has been changed, but she won't give it another chance. I can't believe she has the nerve to tell *me* that my best friend should be Jesus. *Jesus!*"

"I'm not religious, but I know one thing for sure," Alyssa cautioned, "and that is you can't be the savior of your marriage. If she won't try again, it's out of your control, and you need to let go, or else you or her—or both of you—will go completely crazy."

I was offended by the assertion that I was trying to be Rebecca's savior, but she had a point: I was spinning my wheels and getting nowhere but more depressed—just as I had our whole marriage.

It is said everyone has a breaking point. I finally hit mine. Having lost faith in everyone and everything, I resigned myself (again) to the reality of divorce and accepted there was nothing I could do to change Rebecca's mind, let alone redeem myself. I also decided my epiphanies about God, love, and happiness were just figments of false hope. I decided happiness was a liar, and that Rebecca was just another misguided lemming.

I was done with advice, opinions, and self-help. I was done with positive prayers and optimism. I was done with the idea of "playing from the heart" for anyone. And I was done hoping God would help me.

In an effort to find some semblance of normalcy, I tried my best to stay busy and keep my mind clear of anything even remotely relationship-oriented. I even tried mindful meditation again and made it a full five minutes and found it helped me relax. But no matter what I did I couldn't escape the sinking feeling that due to my inability to redeem myself I was destined for proverbial wilderness wandering the rest of my days.

Faithless and hopeless, I became depressed again, stopped taking calls from friends, and only talked to people at work. I crawled into a dark shell and stayed inside unless the kids were over. All hope seemed lost. Then along came the good Professor again.

Reflections

The day after my Labor Day revelations I woke up thinking I could somehow redeem myself and atone for my transgressions. Given the miraculously-timed chain of events I was certain God had sent them for the purpose of changing Rebecca's heart and restoring our marriage.

I was shocked to find she not only didn't believe me but had the audacity to suggest Jesus should be my best friend—as if my entire belief system was in need of an overhaul. Due to my life-long conditioning, I believed "being friends with Jesus" was a lie spun by opportunistic grifters, and I couldn't believe she had fallen for it.

Notably, my friend Aaron had once again given me sound Biblical counsel, and I had once again written it off because it didn't align with my purposes and plan. That, and my self-deterministic mind raged against the idea that God fought battles for people. I was still in warrior mode, fighting for my life to survive and trying to justify and redeem myself, as I had my whole life.

When I finally hit my breaking point, I lost faith in everything—at least that's what I told myself. I suppose it was just easier to believe I had simply been dealt a bad hand in life than continue to bang my head against the wall searching in vain for answers that might not even exist.

I was officially done. And paradoxically, beyond my ability to perceive or comprehend, that was exactly where I needed to be for what was about to happen next.

14: Who Do You Believe?

"You do not realize now what I am doing, but later you will understand." -John 13:7 (NIV)

Mark: I was out for a walk when my phone started vibrating. *Bzzzzz. Bzzzzz.* I grimaced when I saw the caller ID: *Mateo, Heart Strings Music.*

If You Can Believe This

Ugh, I thought. He probably wants me to come back for another lesson so he can preach about his hippie music therapy stuff again. I decided I needed to tell him once and for all to leave me alone, so I answered the phone.

"Hello, Mateo—"

"Mr. Mark. How are you, my brother?"

"Hey listen—"

"How have you been?"

"Not bad," I lied. "Hey so—"

"Man, I was thinking about you yesterday when I was trying to record some music on my keyboard," he laughed heartily. "I need a copy of your learning manual when you're done writing it, I need help with my keyboard! Not everyone is a gifted teacher. I'm so glad you're sharing your gift of music and technology with others!" It struck me he was as eager a student as he was a teacher.

His words were so uplifting and disarming that I couldn't bring myself to tell him to go away. I hadn't ever thought of the book I was writing as a gift, or myself as a gifted teacher, nor had anyone who knew about the book other than my parents been so supportive of it.

"Well, thanks," I said.

"So hey, how are those piano exercises coming along?" he asked.

"Well, I've been working through a rough patch in life, so I haven't had much time for the piano."

"Oh, I'm sorry to hear that, is everything OK?"

"Well, I'm going through a uh... divorce... but it's just about final so..."

"*Woooooooow,*" he said dramatically. "I'm so sorry to hear that Mark, wow. That's a very traumatic and painful event. When is your divorce final?"

"Couple more weeks."

"Wow if you don't mind me asking, are you and your wife Christians?"

Whoa. My religion was a very private matter, and I rarely discussed it with anyone. "Uh, well... I mean... we took Christian vows, so yeah we're believers, why?"

"Mark, *if you can believe this,* I'm a Christian minister and a marriage counselor!" he exalted, as if he had just revealed exciting news I had been eagerly awaiting.

In retrospect it was a miraculous turn of events, but I was so shut down it was lost on me. "That's interesting, but save your breath," I warned. "My ex has already moved on, and I'm over it. We have irreconcilable differences, and our marriage is totally unsalvageable."

"Ohhh, OK, no worries, no stress, I understand," he said, as if the matter was suddenly settled. "Anyway, the reason I called is because I'm excited to tell you I moved into a new studio and would love for you to come and see it tomorrow. I was also hoping to pick your brain a little about my web site, since I know you have a technology background. I'll even buy lunch. What do you say?"

As much as I didn't want to socialize, I felt a tug on my heart to see him again—that, and my conscience told me it was the least I could do after all the time he spent with me on the piano. "Uh, yeah, I can meet for a few," I gave in.

"Awesome!" he cheered, "OK my brother, I will be praying for your heart. See you tomorrow."

It was weird hearing a man say he was going to pray for me. That was a new one, and I didn't know how I felt about it.

Just One Question

The next day I woke up feeling gloomy and wishing I hadn't agreed to meet with him. I grumbled under my breath the whole way to his new studio and vowed not to engage in any warm and fuzzy conversation about music, hearts, relationships, marriage, etc. Me and my plans.

He greeted me out in the parking lot with an even bigger hug than the first time we met and said repeatedly how good it was to see me. It may sound strange, but no one had ever been that welcoming and happy to see me before, and it lifted my spirits so much I forgot about my despair briefly.

Beaming with joy he opened the door to his new studio and ushered me in. It was a beautiful space, and its soft incandescent light and rich earth tones were as warm and welcoming as his bear hugs. I had never observed a teacher take that much care to make their learning space so clean, orderly, and welcoming.

The only thing that seemed to be out of place was a big suitcase on the floor in the corner. I thought to ask him about it, but before I could, he was showing me his web site and seeking my counsel, so I never got a chance.

When we finished discussing his web site, he insisted I show him my progress on the Hanon piano exercises he had given me previously. I reluctantly gave in. Then came another surprise.

As I fumbled through the exercises, he clapped his hands in rhythm and coached me to stay in time with him (which I was unable to do), like I was his student. After I finished, he stressed the importance of "listening to the rhythm and practicing everything in time."

Then he abruptly changed the subject. "So hey I'm really sorry to hear about your marriage, but just one question: why do you think it's unsalvageable?"

Ugh. He went there. "How much time do you have?" I groaned.

"I have all day, my brother," he said.

"Let's just call it a 14-year slow-motion train wreck," I lamented, echoing my friend James' description of my back injury. "We tried to save it repeatedly, but it got to the point where it was so toxic that we couldn't handle it and divorced. But then..."

"But then what?" he pried.

"But then I got injured and humbled... then some other things happened, and I had an epiphany that I hadn't really given my heart to my wife... that I had only been, as you said, playing for myself instead of others... and that I hadn't been following God's way in life... so I apologized to her and said I wanted to try again... but she said it's too late... which is outrageous because she claims to be going to church now... so... I just can't fight anymore..."

"Wow, I had no idea you were going through this," he said sympathetically. "You have been carrying a tremendous burden. But *man,* that epiphany about your heart and following God is a great blessing from God, wow. God has softened your heart. He must have amazing plans for you! Wow."

"*Blessing? Amazing plans?*" I laughed cynically. "I'm getting divorced! How do you figure?"

He looked totally puzzled. "How do you know for sure you're getting divorced?"

"Because she said so."

"Wait, who gave *her* the final say?"

I was confused by his bizarre line of questioning. "I have no idea where you're going with this," I said in frustration.

At that he picked up a Bible that was on his desk, held it up and said solemnly, "I don't know what Bible you read, but *my* Bible says God has supreme power, and *all things* are possible for the one who believes. So that means your marriage isn't over unless God says it is. So *who do you believe*: your wife's word or God's word?"

"I don't think you understand," I countered. "This is our seventh breakup and she doesn't want to try anymore."

"*Wow,* that's an amazing testimony of perseverance!" he said boisterously.

"What are you talking about?"

"Well, you said you *broke up* seven times, but what I heard is that you *persevered* seven times. Most people don't even persevere after the *first* breakup. I'm proud of you and your wife for fighting for your marriage. You're a great inspiration."

I had to pause to process his words because no one had ever portrayed our embarrassing marriage in such a positive light—let alone said it inspired them. I couldn't get my mind around it.

Then I got real and said, "An inspiration? No, when you keep doing the same thing and expecting a different result it's called *insanity*. We didn't inspire anyone. Most people think we're *crazy*."

"Oh, that's understandable," he said casually. "It's not *normal* to see couples fighting through pain to stay together. But the way of God is perseverance. Why? Because perseverance is the character of Christ, and through our trials we are forged into gold. Remember this always: the race is not given to the fast or the strong, but to those who endure until the end. It's just that we need God's strength to do it, we can't do it on our own strength.

Have you been trying to do it on your own strength, or God's?"

Just One Condition

"That's interesting," I said, ignoring his question. "But trust me all hope is lost because I've tried everything, and I can't make her happy, and her mind is made up."

He responded so quick it was like he knew what I was going to say before I said it. "Hope is never lost when God is involved my brother, but you're right about one thing: you didn't make her heart, and she didn't make yours, so you can't *make* each other happy. Only your Savior can do that. And since you're Christian I assume you both believe Jesus is your savior, yes?"

His question caught me off guard because I never equated Jesus with fulfillment of heart and happiness before. I only knew Jesus as the persecuted martyr up on the cross at church. In my mind He was a tragic figure to be revered, mourned, and adored from a reverent distance. Mateo was suggesting a personal savior... like Rebecca, Aaron, and the author of the positive mindset book had. And it still rubbed me all wrong.

But! On second thought, Rebecca and I had been trying to be each other's happiness saviors for years and failing over and over. In fact, our failure to fulfill each other's happiness, to complete each other, was one of the main reasons we were divorcing. Suddenly the personal savior idea wasn't so crazy after all. Then came some of the most alien words I've ever heard.

"I'm glad *my* wife knows Jesus is her Savior and the voice of truth!" he said dramatically, pretending to wipe perspiration from his forehead. "When I asked her to marry me, she said yes on one condition: if I accepted she would always love Jesus more than she loved me ha ha. I said no problem, because my back isn't strong enough to carry all your hope and happiness. I can't even carry mine!"

Whoa. Due to my conditioning it was hard to comprehend Mateo, a man of such great knowledge, confidence, and talent, could be so... dependent... on *Jesus...* and so... proud of it. I couldn't get my mind around it.

But as hard as I tried, I couldn't deny the fact that I had been carrying my hope and happiness burdens (and Rebecca's) my whole life, and sure enough I had run out of strength—figuratively and literally.

"Hmm, that part about heavy burdens resonates with me," I intimated, almost under my breath, "especially since we've both suffered bad back injuries."

Supreme, Uncontested Power

"Really? Wow! I'm not surprised," he said, as he put the Bible back. "Carrying heavy burdens is one of the main ways the enemy divides husband and wife. But that doesn't mean your marriage is unsalvageable. Do you believe the Biblical word of truth that God has the supreme and uncontested power to save your marriage?"

"Well, it's hard to believe when my ex is so stuck in her ways and adamant about divorcing," I said. "Not only that, she's a hypocrite. She actually had the nerve to tell me that Jesus should be my best friend... as she's in the process of throwing a divorce party! How Biblical is *that*?"

At that he suddenly lit up and laughed loudly. "Hey, she's right about Jesus being your best friend ha ha! I like her! She's preaching good! Sometimes the truth rides in on the back of donkey!"

What? I was outraged he took her side and totally glossed over her appalling hypocrisy. I sighed heavily and shook my head in resignation. I was thinking I should leave again.

"Mark let me tell you something," he said in a consoling voice. "You might not want to hear this right now, but it sounds like your wife is seeking truth, and I think God might be working on her heart and leading her to the Cross for reconciliation. You never know, he might be working on your heart, too"

"Somehow I doubt it," I said. "She just told me she's not in love with me anymore. It's a waste of time. I'm wise enough to know that when you realize you're riding a dead horse, the best strategy is to dismount."

At that he scrunched up his face like he smelled something foul. "Who told you *that*? That's not Biblical truth. The Bible says, 'the heart is deceitful above all things,' and no one but God can understand it.' So you couldn't possibly know what's *really* in your wife's heart. The *horse*, as you called it, is only dead if you stop putting your hope in God to save it." -Jeremiah 17:9 (NIV)

"But I did put my hope in God," I insisted. "I saw the signs from Him. I prayed, apologized, and begged her for forgiveness. And all I got was more rejection. I had to give up because there's nothing more I can do, and I was going crazy."

"Hmmm," he replied, like a doctor pondering a patient's symptoms. "Well the spirit of God is a sound mind, so if you're going crazy you might be doubting His power. The Bible says a man who doubts is 'double-minded and unstable in all his ways.' Hey, maybe God doesn't want you to do anything more right now except be still and *believe.*" -James 1:8 (ESV)

"I've tried to believe. But I also believe God only helps those who help themselves."

"Nope, that's not true either," he quickly refuted me. "We are saved by grace and faith my brother. The Bible says, 'God has mercy and compassion on whoever He chooses,' even wretched sinners like me and you. And I'm sure glad for that because if He didn't, man, phew, I would be a mess." -Romans 9:15 (NIV)

I didn't like being referred to as a "wretched sinner," but it struck me he was proposing the same thing the author of my positive mindset book proposed: that God's help, even His favor, wasn't a response to people's good works or good intentions, but because He loved them, and they had faith in Him.

Then he dropped another bomb when he added, "The Bible says, 'God is love, and love bears all things, believes all things, and never fails with faith,' so who do you

believe is the voice of truth: God or your wife?" -1
Corinthians 13:7 (NIV)

That question rocked me. It was the moment I realized
I didn't look to the Bible as definitive truth, and I took
more stock in my wife's words than God's. I had never
looked to the Bible to define *love* either. It was one thing
to recite Bible verses to gain a positive mindset and so
forth, but to define love? I couldn't grasp it. I thought,
*Either Professor Heart Strings is totally delusional, or I
have been profoundly misled my whole life,* and I wasn't
sure which was the case.

After a period of awkward silence, he asked if he could
"pray over me." It was another alien idea since I was under
the belief that only authorized clergy prayed for people,
but I didn't see how it could hurt.

Then he put his hands on my shoulders and prayed I
would surrender to God's uncontested power, follow the
voice of truth, and "let go and let God's will be done."
And he prayed for divine healing and reconciliation.

I had never heard such kind, loving, and compassionate
words, let alone prayers for my benefit before. I was so
humbled I could barely say "amen." Then he added,
"Don't ever forget the effectual fervent prayer of a
righteous man availeth much." -James 5:16

We parted company with another one of his big
embraces. I think it was the first time I actually hugged
him back. Despite my resistance to his teachings, I was so
grateful that someone finally understood the weight of the
burdens I had been carrying and appeared to want to help

me get out from under them. I was so choked up I could only wave as I got into my car.

When I shut the door, he motioned for me to roll down the window. When I did, he said, "One more thing."

"What's that?"

"Fake it 'til you make it."

"What do you mean?" I asked, as I turned the key and the engine roared to life.

"Your faith," he said, clasping his hands together in a praying position. "Fake it 'til you make it."

Reflections

As the Bible says, "God's ways are higher than our ways than the heavens are from the earth." (Isaiah 55:8). I never dreamed Mateo would turn out to be a Christian minister who not only knew the Word of God but believed it and lived it—to the extent that he knew it and played it by heart like he played the piano.

Among the many seeds of truth he planted that day, three of the most compelling were that 1) We are saved by God's grace and our faith, and that God helps us simply because He loves us, not because we do good works for Him; 2) That Rebecca and I could not be each other's saviors, and only Jesus could complete our hearts and bring us fulfilling happiness; and 3) That a man who doubts God is double-minded and unstable in all his ways.

Not that I believed those things right away. It was one thing to believe God's word had power to improve my mindset; it was quite another to believe Jesus was not only the deliverer from damnation but the divine Captain of the heart and source of fulfillment for all humanity—and marriages.

Encouraged by his friendship, but opposed to his ideas, I was tempted to ditch Mateo again. But strangely I couldn't. Because beneath all my frustration and unbelief, there was an increasingly louder inner voice ministering to my heart, "Listen to his words. Follow his lead. He knows the way out of the wilderness."

The *Last* Breakup

15: Who Do You Follow?

"But the wisdom from above is first pure, then peaceable, gentle, open to reason, full of mercy and good fruits, impartial and sincere." -James 3:17 (ESV)

Mark: After the second meeting with Mateo, I was deeply torn again. On one hand, my heart was stirred by his encouraging, authoritative Biblical wisdom and unbending, inspirational belief; on the other, seeing Rebecca moving on with her life and hearing her promise to never reconcile again made it difficult to believe God would turn things around if I would just believe in His power.

As I aggravated over those things, I received an email from Mateo titled "I Believe! Help My Unbelief." It was a Bible story I had never heard before about how a man asked Jesus if He could perform a miracle to heal His son, and Jesus replied, "If I *can*? Of course I can. All things are possible for those who believe." Then the man exclaimed, "I believe! Help my unbelief," and Jesus immediately healed His son. -Mark 9:23 (NIV)

Mateo wrote under the Scripture: "Mark, all things are possible through Jesus if you believe. It's not a matter of whether God can save your marriage or not. Of course He can. He parted the Red Sea, resurrected Jesus from the dead, and gave us eternal life. What matters is if you *believe* He can. I believe He can. Do you?"

I wanted to reply, "no," but I couldn't—unless I was willing to call Jesus a liar and the Bible a fraud.

Then at the very end of the email Mateo added, "Can't wait to meet with you again. You're making amazing progress on those Hanons! ((Smile))."

The Voice of Truth

Still skeptical of his beliefs, but lifted by his friendship and encouragement, I returned to Mateo's studio for another round of piano lessons at his behest. Within moments of arriving he asked me to play the Hanon exercises again and said, "The stage is yours."

It was once again showtime, but strangely I didn't feel as fearful as I did before. In fact, to my surprise, as I awkwardly labored through the exercises and tried to keep time with him (as he clapped his hands rhythmically and chanted, "*stay... in... time... Mark... play... on... the... beat!*"), I actually felt strangely joyful and even laughed at my mistakes.

Nevertheless, when the lesson was over, I hoped to make a quick exit because I wasn't in the mood to discuss the "unbelief" email he sent. But of course, before I could get on my way he asked, "One question before you leave my brother: do you believe all things are possible?"

I sighed. "Look, I believe in God, I just don't see how He can change a person who is shut down and doesn't think they need to change."

"I told you, God can do *anything*," he said matter of factly. "You just have to have a little faith."

"I've tried, but it's hard."

"It's only hard for the same reason you struggle to keep time with my voice when you're playing the Hanons.

It's hard for the same reason you can't play jazz yet. You haven't learned the fundamentals and principles of *faith*, and you haven't practiced them. If you did, you would know the voice of Truth, which is the voice of Jesus, and you would believe it and follow it." (John 10:27)

"How do I get to know the voice of Truth?" I asked incredulously.

"How did you get to know your own son's voice so you could tell it was him if he called out to you from a playground full of kids?"

"I spend a lot of time with him... and..." I stopped mid-sentence when I realized what I was saying.

"Exactly," he said with a smile, "and that's how you come to know the Truth and believe too. The Bible says, 'faith comes by hearing the message about Christ.' The Bible also says, 'man cannot live on bread alone but by every word that proceedeth out of the mouth of God.' (Romans 10:17; Matthew 4:4)

"Mark, if you repent and put your faith in Jesus, the Holy Spirit of Truth will be in your heart and testify the Truth to you, and you will stop doubting and have faith."

I still struggled to grasp it. "Obviously I have a lot to learn about the Bible," I confessed, "but I'm telling you, she's totally off on another road, living a whole new life, and there's no chance of her having a change of heart."

"Not true" he reproved me. "First of all, only God truly knows her heart because He made it, so you don't really know the truth in her heart. Second, it doesn't matter what she is doing or planning. God is *sovereign*. Do you know what that means? It means He is *all* powerful, and if God wants something to happen, there is nothing anyone, including you, can do to stop it." -1 Corinthians 7:14 (NIV)

Foreign Language

"OK," I conceded, "but even if that's true, you *must* admit some people have irreconcilable differences and are just not meant to be! Look at—"

"No, I don't admit that at all," he said firmly. "That's the voice of the world talking, not the voice of God's true word. The word of God says, 'God can do *all* things, and that no *purpose* of His can be thwarted.'" -Job 42:2 (ESV)

"But—"

"You saw the email I sent you right?" he interrupted. "What did Jesus say when the disciples asked Him why they couldn't heal the little boy?"

I couldn't remember. He answered his own question. "He said 'because... of... your... *unbelief.*' Mark, all things are possible only for those who *believe*."

"I don't think you understand," I insisted. "Even if she were to somehow undergo a change of heart, we have grown so far apart that I don't see how we could ever coexist harmoniously."

He nodded sympathetically and said, "But I *do* understand... and so does God. That's why He sent Jesus to save us from our sins and give us the desire to love Him and each other as He loves us. God is love, my brother.

"Haven't you heard? Men and women are like Mars and Venus. The only way they can join together, play from the same sheet of music, and make beautiful love songs together is with the love of God through Jesus in their hearts.

"Jesus is the only conductor who can take two vastly different sounds like a white key and a black key on a piano and fuse them together into one harmonious sound like a music chord... like the Bible says: a 'cord of three strands'!" (Ecclesiastes 4:12)

"It's hard to imagine," I said.

"It used to be hard for me to imagine too," he confessed. "But I can tell you this, if my wife and I didn't follow Jesus together, we wouldn't have the amazing friendship and marriage we have. We would be divorced a long time ago. Without the love of God, we are just two clanging cymbals ha ha. We have to surrender our wills every day together to Him."

I was once again at a loss for words. I had never heard the idea that "surrendering" to God was the key to harmonious marriage; nor had I ever heard a man literally boast about his "amazing friendship" with his wife.

In my world, love between men and woman was limited to duty, sex, and romance. Having a "music making" relationship with Rebecca was not in the realm of possibilities.

Then he added, "Aside from Jesus, my wife is my first priority, you know why? Because God commands me to love my wife as Christ loves the church. Do you know what that means? It means to love her so much that I'm willing to lay down my life for her, just like Jesus laid down His life for us. When Jesus died for our sins, He literally took a bullet for us so we could have eternal life. When you were with Rebecca would you have taken a bullet for her?" (Ephesians 5:25; John 15:13)

I had never considered my love for Rebecca in such dramatic life-and-death terms before. "I don't see how that's possible when she's so... hard to love..."

"Well Mark," he said patiently, "I'm hard to love too. I can be demanding, controlling, impatient, grouchy, stubborn—oh and hypocritical—just to name a few. But my wife submits to God, and He blesses her with His *grace* to keep bearing with me, even when I'm at my worst. That's how I am able to bear with her too. Grace comes only one way, and that's by staying connected to the vine of Jesus, my brother."

"Well good for you," I said dismissively. "But I still don't see how it's possible when there's so much pain, baggage, and resentment."

"Oh, it's *not* possible without GRACE," he said passionately. "But with grace and faith in Jesus *all* things are possible. The Holy Spirit is the great physician of the heart. When He enters, grace and truth enter, and He heals old wounds, removes heavy baggage burdens, and gives us a new hearts and supernatural strength to forgive and love each other as God forgives and loves us." (Philippians 4:13; Matthew 11:28; Ezekiel 36:26)

"That sounds good in theory," I argued, "but trust me, she's closed off and doesn't open her heart to anyone."

At that he smiled warmly and paused for effect. "Are you sure you're not describing *yourself?* Because I've noticed you seem to struggle with opening up also. Is that fair to say?"

He was right: I hated "opening up." In my world, life was essentially a dog-eat-dog poker game and real men—wise men—didn't ever reveal their "cards" (as in their deepest thoughts, feelings, etc.), lest they get taken advantage of. I finally grumbled, "Uh, I guess, sort of, but this isn't about me."

At that he leaned forward and said, "But it *is* about you... and me. God calls us men to be the head of our marriages. That means we're supposed to open our hearts and submit, obey the truth, and lead by servant-hearted example, like Christ, with faith. The Bible says, 'those who are last and the servant of all will be first.' When you lead with God's love, your wife will follow with God's love. That is God's marriage design." -Mark 9:35 (NIV)

Even though I had witnessed an example of a servant-hearted man out my front window in my neighbor Matt and felt a new desire to serve my wife and family, I shuddered at the thought of becoming an "open-hearted" pansy. The words "servant" and "submit" made me cringe.

To be sure, his soliloquy of softness was an assault on my identity as a man. In my mind, I was an artist, a warrior, an athlete, a business executive... not a doormat servant. It was a hard-enough challenge to just follow God's rules, let alone give up my manhood. Then he went a step further.

"Some guys get weirded out when I say I'm whipped for my wife," he admitted proudly. "But that's only because they don't know the word of God, which says, 'husbands must love their wives as they love their own bodies, and he who loves his wife loves himself.' How many men do you think love their wives as much as they love their own bodies ha ha?" -Ephesians 5:28 (NIV)

"Not many," he answered his own question. "They think submitting and serving makes them soft, but actually in God's eyes it makes them real men, like Jesus, and it pleases Him greatly. I don't know about you, but I live to please God, not people."

Admittedly my ego raged against the idea of "submitting" to my wife, or anyone for that matter. In the cool guy, macho world where I resided for so long, being "whipped" was pure sacrilege and treason to the male species.

"Uh, no, when I hear the word 'submission,' I think of being in chains," I said in a disapproving tone.

Instructions for Christian Households

"That's common. I used to think the same," he replied matter-of-factly. "But that's because in our culture we aren't taught the Biblical meaning of marriage submission. Most guys think it means to be a slave. That's not what it means. It means to lead with love and to serve, encourage, and build up our wives. That's grace."

Then he added, "When husband and wife submit to God, the Holy Spirit in their hearts neutralizes their natural opposition to each other and unites them in spiritual harmony. That's what God's word, the voice of Truth, is referring to when it says, 'The two will become one flesh.'" -Mark 10:8 (NIV)

"I don't know," I said. "Every time I've ever been submissive, people see it as weakness and take advantage of me."

"Man, you sound like you've been burned by love," he observed. "You're right, it *is* a sign of weakness in our macho culture. But the Bible says, 'God's power is made *perfect* in our weakness.' So as crazy as it might sound, the more we submit, the more wisdom and courage He gives us to protect our hearts and love others as He loves us." -2 Corinthians 12:9 (NIV)

He then grabbed his Bible again, rapidly flipped through it until he found what he was looking for and read aloud, "Instructions for Christian Households. Husbands and wives, *Submit* to one another out of reverence for Christ." (Ephesians 5:21-25)

Then he said, "Notice God commands us to submit to our wives out of reverence for *Jesus*. I worship Jesus, then I have His love and desire to love my wife and vice versa. Does that make sense?"

"I guess," I said. "It goes against everything I know, and I don't know if I could do it myself, but I understand."

At that he smiled knowingly and said, "Good news my brother, you don't have to do it yourself. God will give you the *power* to conquer, just like He did for Joseph, Joshua, and Jesus!

"You just have to submit your will, *obey God's commandments,* and have faith, and the Holy Spirit will give you real strength and endurance to do things you can't do on your own. I'm talking about the power of *grace* to meet your wife where she is rather than where you *think* she should be. Then you will go last as the servant of all, and grace will be multiplied in your marriage."

Given his passion and confidence, it was hard not to believe him. But the idea of "submitting to Jesus" and harnessing some kind of supernatural power to be the love leader of my marriage was so alien that I couldn't grasp it. I also couldn't grasp ever gaining Rebecca's love, honor, and respect. It just seemed… impossible.

Evidently, he sensed my resistance because he went on to tell me that it was OK if I didn't believe right away, that I should keep seeking the truth, and that I should pray for a "heart of understanding and obedience" so I could be reconciled with God through Christ.

"If you become friends with Jesus, you'll become friends with God," he assured me. "Then you'll know God's love, and it will totally transform you. Then you will learn to follow God's way, the example of Christ, instead of yours, and God will give you the heart to fulfill your Biblical role in marriage and much more. You will become a new creation. An entirely new man."

It sounded like a delusional fairy tale, yet in some bizarre way that I couldn't explain it agreed with my soul and even gave me a tiny bit of hope.

After we finished up, he hugged me, high-fived me, and reminded me to keep believing in God's power, even if every voice in my life was trying to convince me to believe otherwise. He said, "The word of God is the only thing that NEVER changes. You can bet your life on it."

When I got home, I checked my emails. There was another from Mateo titled "How Joseph moved mountains." It was a Bible story about a man in the Old Testament who was sold into slavery by his own envious brothers, falsely accused and imprisoned, but whose heart remained submitted and "obedient" to God. Consequently, in time God delivered him from slavery, raised him into a position of power and nobility, gave him power to forgive his brothers, and ultimately saved his family.

At the end of the email Mateo added, "Mark, Joseph loved God above all others—even himself—and was rewarded for his obedient heart and faith. He is a great role model for us men because he obeyed and followed God first. Who do *you* follow first?"

I wanted to reply, "God!" but I couldn't. The story about Joseph was a humbling and humiliating reminder that I didn't know God's word at all except for the popular verses and the Lord's Prayer. I had followed everyone and everything *but* God.

As I closed his email, I recalled the prayer I said to God after reading the convicting verses about sin and punishment in Jeremiah. I had asked God to show me His way because I didn't know it. It occurred to me that in some incredible twist of divine fate Mateo was God's answer to my prayer. He was not only teaching me about marriage, but how to follow God... even how to be a real man in the eyes of God.

The only problem was, I didn't like the way of God he was teaching me. Submission and obedience ran opposed to my self-sufficient warrior mindset—not to mention my entire idea of manhood. I also couldn't fathom how Rebecca could ever, in any universe, come to love and respect me as Mateo described. If that wasn't a tall enough mountain to scale, I couldn't imagine surrendering my entire identity to become a "servant of all"... for anyone.

Reflections

After that meeting I found myself facing another perplexing conundrum. Even though Mateo's teachings about opening up, servant-hearted leadership, and multiplying grace were totally alien to me, I couldn't argue because he was gleaning them right from the Bible—that and the fact he was personifying them through his own servant-hearted ministry and inspiring me to reciprocate.

But of the many seeds of truth he planted that day, the most important was the power and supremacy of Jesus. Namely that only Jesus had the power to heal Rebecca's heart, only Jesus could give us the power to forgive and love each other and save our marriage, only Jesus could give me the soft heart of a servant-hearted leader, and only Jesus (not basketball or anything else) could remove the deep-seated angst and restlessness that I was coming to see had cursed me since a very young.

And truth be told, that was one of my biggest stumbling blocks because I just couldn't comprehend how

Jesus, the man I had seen depicted so many times throughout my life as persecuted, emaciated, crushed under the weight of the Cross, or hanging from it, could help me. But that's only because I didn't yet know *the power*.

The *Last* Breakup

16: Power Surge

"For God gave us a spirit not of fear but of power and love and of sound mind." -2 Timothy 1:7 (ESV)

Mark: Despite my ongoing unbelief, I was uplifted by Mateo's friendship and belief in me, and it gave me confidence and a small bit of hope for the future. It was around that time I finally completed and published my keyboard learning manual book for musicians and began practicing the Hanon piano exercises daily.

That's not to say all was well with my soul. With less than two weeks to go until our divorce was finalized, and no contact with Rebecca at all, I still mourned the loss of my marriage and family, blamed myself for our collapse, and couldn't fathom the idea that God could move mountains of baggage to save us.

But even with all those burdens weighing me down, there was still a flicker of hope in my heart that Mateo's powerful Bible teachings (including that my heart and soul could be well with God, regardless of the outcome of my marriage) were true.

It was with that tiny seed of faith I kept hunting for truth to validate everything I had been learning about the power of God... and prayed to God to help my unbelief.

And then…

Power Couple

One Sunday, a week and a half before our divorce was set to be finalized, I was compelled to hire some gardeners from Craig's List to clean up my backyard vegetation. It had grown unwieldy during my summer of discontent and was in desperate need of maintenance.

The gardeners were a husband and wife team named Art and Maria, and from the moment we shook hands I knew there was something special about them. I started to get a sense of what it was as I showed them around the backyard, and Art used words such as "blessings" and "gifts" to teach me about the trees and shrubs and explain their landscaping "restoration" process. He spoke of plant life in a spiritual way like Mateo spoke of music.

Pointing to a Eucalyptus Tree he said, "Be careful with that one, sometimes they fail to develop deep roots, and can be vulnerable to storms." I recalled the Scripture in Jeremiah about the necessity of being deeply rooted in God's love.

Then I watched in awe as Art and his wife worked in perfect harmony with every landscaping tool I'd ever seen (and some I hadn't) to transform the overgrown jungle in my backyard into a beautiful landscape worthy of a magazine cover. I recalled reading an article a ways back about how Jesus restored man's relationship with God, and I felt a powerful tug on my heart.

When they finished their work, we gathered on the back patio and drank a cold beverage together. They said they had been married and in business together for over 30 years, and that their work was a "labor of love." Curious to know their secret I asked, "So if you had to attribute your marriage success to one thing what would it be?"

They looked at each other, looked back at me, and answered in unison, "Jesus."

Holy... I couldn't believe my ears. "That's... amazing," I whispered in awe.

Then Art proceeded to play every string of my heart like a master musician. "When we accepted Jesus as our Lord and Savior and followed His way, God blessed us with the power to love each other with mercy and grace and have a friendship we never had before." Miraculously, his was almost the same exact testimony as Mateo's.

I was so overwhelmed with joyful awe that I was moved to share my story with them. I said, "That's truly amazing because my wife and I are going through a divorce, and a Christian minister recently told me the same thing you just did about Jesus and marriage. The minister has actually been trying to convince me that my marriage can be saved, but I just don't believe there's any hope."

Art's face lit up. "There's hope! Maria and I almost divorced once too!" he nearly shouted in joy.

Maria nodded in agreement and added, "We were torn apart and at war with each other, but then we gave our lives to Jesus, followed His way, and received *the power.*"

"The power?" I asked.

"Yes, *resurrection power,* that comes from the Holy Spirit after we submit, repent, and follow Jesus," Art testified passionately. "Only the Holy Spirit can give our hearts the desire to love and *forgive* each other like God loves and forgives us. Only through Jesus is true peace and harmony between husband and wife possible."

It was a miracle. He was saying the same exact thing that Mateo had said: If Rebecca and I surrendered and followed the way of Jesus, God would give us the power and desire to love and forgive each other, and we would no longer be at war. That was the first time it occurred to me that forgiveness was the one thing Rebecca and I could never fully do.

Before Art and Maria departed, they prayed for me, Rebecca, and our marriage. Then to my shock Art prayed for belief and reconciliation. "Father bless Mark and Rebecca with the belief in the resurrection power of Christ to heal their hearts and bless their marriage with abundant grace and immovable faith. In Jesus name." Then they gave me a big Mateo-sized hug and told me to "Keep the faith" before they drove away.

As I walked back inside with tears in my eyes it hit me Art and Maria personified the forgiving, healing, reconciling, and harmonizing love in Christ Mateo had preached to me about, and I wondered if they were the kind of couple Rebecca had met at her church.

Then came another knee-buckling revelation when I realized God's love was the glue that bound Mateo and Art's marriages together as one, and if Rebecca and I surrendered to Jesus, God's love could bind our hearts together as one too.

Suddenly my spirit was filled with hope again.

Mic Drop

Blown away by the miraculous encounter and revelation truth, and certain they were signs that God was going to reconcile our marriage, I texted Rebecca and said, "You won't believe this! I just met a couple at my house who have been married 30 years and say their marriage was saved by Jesus. This is a sign. Jesus is the missing link to our marriage. If we follow His way, we can have an amazing marriage."

Her disheartening response came a little later: "Stop this madness. Move on. It's over."

Once again, I felt my hope fade like a stage light after the final scene of a tragic play. The end.

Then my indignation turned towards Mateo. *I should have never even told him about my divorce,* I seethed. *If it wasn't for him, I would have moved on by now. He's the reason I just got thrown under the bus again. I should've never even connected with him after our first meeting.*

I decided to call him on the phone and give him a piece of my mind. When he answered, I told him about the gardeners and how Rebecca rejected me again. Then I grumbled, "See what happens when I try to submit? I get walked all over! I hope you can see now that some people can't be changed, and some marriages can't be salvaged. It is what it is. If all these miracles don't convince her to come home, *nothing* will."

His response was exasperating as always. "Phew! I'm glad she said no to coming back home."

"Wait what? *Why?*"

"Because I haven't been praying for her to go home. I've been praying for her to go to Jesus."

"*What?* What do you mean? How can she—"

He interrupted. "*Mark*, this is what I've been trying to get you to see. Her heart is still hard. She doesn't trust you, and she doesn't believe your marriage can be saved. You... can't... change... her... heart.

"Listen closely to me. It doesn't matter how convincing you are or how many miracles you witness. If you get back together before you both go to Jesus to be saved, your marriage will fail an *eighth* time."

"Oh, come on!" I bellowed in protest.

"Your pride won't like this," he counseled me firmly, "but Rebecca doesn't need you. She needs Jesus. You don't need her. You need Jesus. You both need to hear the voice of Truth. He is our shepherd and the voice of mercy, grace, forgiveness, and healing. Only He has the power to save your souls and marriage. And by the way, God cares more about your souls than your marriage, believe it or not."

He was right, I didn't like what he was saying at all, and I almost hung up on him. But then he asked two questions that turned my world upside down. "When are you going to give your wife to Jesus and allow Him to be her Savior? And when are you going to allow Him to be *yours*?"

I was spellbound. Of the many riveting questions he asked, that was the most disturbing and yet at the same time enlightening. It brought me to the instant realization of a truth that had eluded me my whole life: no one belonged to me nor did I belong to anyone else. We all belonged to God... and there was only one Savior... and it was Jesus... and despite my religious beliefs, I had yet to truly surrender my life to Him.

All I could do was listen at that point because I was totally speechless again. Mateo, of course, was overjoyed to keep playing my heart strings with the truth, just he had been doing since we first met.

"To surrender means to open your heart, let go of *your* control, obey God, and let *Him* control. Due to deep-seated trust issues, a lot of people have a *fear* of opening their hearts to God and letting go of control. They fear if they let go and *trust* God, love will fly away and never return. So out of fear they hold on tight and won't let go, and they suffocate love.

"Fear is a liar. Fear is the devil. And his goal is to divorce us from God and each other. But here's the good news. FAITH overpowers fear, and truth overpowers lies. How do we get faith and truth?"

I couldn't believe I could finally answer one of his questions. "God's word?"

"Yes, with the illuminating help of the Holy Spirit!" he said triumphantly. "Mark, you're learning the fundamentals. God's word is truth! Jesus said, 'sanctify them by the truth, your word is truth.' You and your wife need to be sanctified by the truth so you will stop believing the lies from your emotions and other voices in life and only believe God's promises. -John 17:17 (NIV)

"Here's a question to ask yourself: how can your wife hear the truth from her Savior and obey God's will if you are trying to be her voice of truth? Remember what God said to Pharaoh when Pharaoh was controlling the Hebrews in slavery?"

I had no clue.

"He said 'how long will you refuse to *humble yourself* before me? Let my people go, that they may serve me.'" -Exodus 10:3 (NIV)

Ouch. Upon hearing those words, I was overwhelmed with emotion, followed by the sudden realization that not only had I failed to let go, but I didn't even know *how* to let go. Then my heart opened up a tiny bit and out came the truth. "I've tried to let go," I said with a lump in my throat, "I guess I just struggle with... I don't know..." I couldn't find the words.

Mateo found the words for me. "Pride, humility, belief, trust, faith... heh... *grace.* Have no fear brother, we *all* struggle with those things.

"But! Good news. We can do *all* things through Jesus Christ who strengthens us, including let go. We just have to trust God's way is better than ours... even if we have to fake it until it becomes real to us."

Then came the crescendo question of his heart-string-plucking symphony: "So tell me: when will you open your heart, humble yourself, and trust God rather than yourself?"

Mic drop.......................

162

When he asked that question it finally sank in. I couldn't argue anymore. He was right. There was no more denying it: by Biblical definition I was a faithless man (which was truly astonishing given the time I spent in church throughout my life). I had never trusted God. I didn't even know His word. For as long as I could remember, I only trusted myself. I was totally leveled.

Begin by Obeying

Resigned to defeat, I finally confessed, "I don't know how to let go. Battling is all I've ever known. I don't even know where to begin."

"You begin by *obeying* God. Repent and believe in Jesus, then surrender control to God and trust Him. If you seek first God's righteousness, even if your wife doesn't, God will sanctify her. That is a Biblical fact. But more importantly, your soul will get right with God.

"Listen I'm going to send you an email later tonight with an assignment. Will you commit to working on it?" - 1 Corinthians 7:14 (NIV)

I agreed to do his assignment, and he prayed for me again before we disconnected. Later that night his email arrived. It said:

"Trust in the LORD with all your heart; and lean not on your own understanding. In all your ways acknowledge him, and He will direct all your paths." -Proverbs 3:5 (NIV)

Then he wrote, "How do we acknowledge God? We obey Him. We seek first His righteousness. How did Jesus learn obedience? Jesus learned *obedience* from what he *suffered,* from his *perseverance.* How did Jesus persevere? His faith." -Hebrews 5:8 (NIV)

Then at the end of his email he concluded, "Read the Book of Job to learn about obedience and faith. It is through the *fire of trial* that God refines us into gold, just as He did Jesus. Job and Jesus both knew God's word. They <u>treasured</u> God's word. And that's how we also overcome fear and walk by truth, grace, and faith."

Feeling another burst of hope from his encouragement, I spent the next hour reading the Book of Job in my red Bible. Though some of it went over my head, the one thing that leapt off the pages was how Job maintained undying faith in God even as he lay dying and his friends and his wife (!) gave up hope.

"But God knows me, and when he has tried me, I shall come out as <u>gold</u>. My foot has held fast to his steps; I have kept his way and have not turned aside. I have not departed from the commandment of his lips; I have <u>treasured the words of his mouth more than food itself</u>. But he dies as he wills even when I don't understand it, and I trust He will complete his work in me, whatever is in His mind. Therefore, I will continue to have <u>faith</u> in Him and <u>obey</u> Him. And I will continue to praise Him even as darkness covers me..." -Job 23:10 (paraphrased from KJV)

Even as darkness covers me. Wow! It was truly remarkable how Job not only knew God's word but *treasured* it like a precious stone, lived by it, and consequently had the God-granted *power* of faith to persevere through such extraordinary heartbreak and even the unbelief of his wife and friends.

Then came the sobering realization again that the "way of God" I had read about in Jeremiah but didn't understand, was the way of obedient faith... and it was from faith that the blessings of love, peace, sound mind, and inner strength came... and I was a faithless man.

Worse, I was a vain, rivalrous, doubter and scoffer whose hope and heart were in myself and the world, not in God. With more tears I prayed to God to show me how to turn my heart to Him, keep His way, and unlock the faith and courage of Job in my own life—not to save my marriage, but to save my own soul. The next day He sent me the key.

Reflections

After the miraculous encounter with the gardeners, I was certain Rebecca would see the light. When she didn't, I was certain that I would put Mateo in his place and prove our marriage couldn't be saved. I was dead wrong on both counts.

It had become a humbling pattern since we separated: Every assumption, prediction, and plan of mine failed. The problem was my faith was still in myself and my own worldly wisdom, and I was still trying to operate on my failing strength rather than surrendering to God and operating on His.

It wasn't until I met the gardeners and heard the message about Christ, heard another one of Mateo's teachings about following the voice of Jesus, and read the book of Job that I began to see God's word wasn't just a book of moral rules or a mind-conditioning tool, but the actual *living truth* and treasure of the hearts of those who loved him and served him—and the actual way of truth and love God wanted me to live.

And that's when I began to see the necessity of "letting go," and, as Mateo said, giving my whole heart (and desire to control Rebecca's) to Jesus, not to be reconciled with Rebecca, but to be reconciled with God.

Rebecca: Only in hindsight can I now see God had revealed to Mark what He had started to reveal to me months before. The great irony is that I was fully convinced Mark was lost and too far gone to be saved, and he was convinced of the same exact thing about me.

It is mind-boggling to see now that God was leading us to the same truths in completely different ways: me through a church and Mark through a music teacher and minister. Even more mind-boggling is that both of us were struggling with the same unbelief challenge at the same time, totally unbeknownst to each other.

17: Moving Mountains

"For nothing will be impossible for God." -Luke 1:37 (ESV)

Mark: The next morning I miraculously woke to bright sunshine in my room, great hope in my heart, and Jesus on my mind. As I prepared for the day, I reflected on the events of the past few months and remembered the first time I *heard* the verse "I can do all things through Christ who strengthens me" in the positive mindset book. It was hard to believe how much my understanding had evolved in such a short time, especially after meeting the gardeners and hearing Jesus was their secret to life and love.

Letting Go, Letting God

I can't recall the exact sequence of events that day, but at some point, the many puzzle pieces of divine truth I had been collecting over the past six months gradually came together to form an image that would forever change my view about life and my purpose in it—let alone love, marriage, and everything else.

The image that came into focus was not of a man atop a mountain, or a man outside my window, or a musician, or a man on TV playing basketball, or a great philosopher, or a celebrated CEO, or a man behind a pulpit. Nor was it an image I saw with my eyes. It was an image I saw and felt in my heart and soul, and it was the image of Jesus Christ.

And at that instant I knew He was the *real man* I wanted to start modeling my life after. I had finally come to believe He alone was the only one in the universe capable of throwing off my heavy baggage burdens, moving my mountains of fear and pride, exorcising my demons, unchaining me from my dependencies, healing my old wounds, softening my heart, and freeing me from the sin and false teachings that had shackled me for so long... and maybe even save our marriage.

Then I thought of the radiant flower springing up from the ashes of the burned-out wilderness again, and realized it signaled new life in Christ, that I was being born again in the Spirit. God had made a way in the wilderness to bring me the truth that would finally set me free, and the truth was Jesus Christ. (Ezekiel 36:26; 2 Corinthians 5:17; John 3:3)

Then I arrived at the heart of the truth when it hit me that to be friends with Jesus was to be friends with God and thus God's love. In that instant of awareness, I was driven to drop to my knees and cry out to Jesus:

"Lord *Jesus*, I surrender my life to you. Please forgive me for my sins and being so rebellious. Teach me to be patient, self-controlled and faithful. Teach me to trust you. Teach me to love like you do. Free me from my fears and the heavy burden to direct and control everything and give me a soft heart of understanding and obedience so I can learn the full truth and know you and God's love. Today I give myself to you, and I give Rebecca to you. Amen."

Truth be told, when I started that confession I did not 100% fully believe what I was saying, and I had no clue how I was going to unlearn all the false worldly teachings that defined me and shed all of my worldly identities. But amazingly, by the time I reached the end, I felt an overwhelming sense of hope, forgiveness, peace, security, and actual freedom, and it made me rejoice, "Thank you, Jesus" for the first time in my life.

I rejoiced with immense new hope that—regardless of whether or not my marriage was saved—God loved me, that Jesus was going to teach me His way and not leave me behind, and that with His strength I would be liberated from the crushing burden of self-sufficiency and the exhausting, fruitless quest for worldly redemption and validation.

And when my inner cynic tried to steal in and raise doubt again, I defiantly prayed from my heart, "Jesus I believe, help my unbelief!" And then I felt the deeply fulfilling and reassuring love of God in my heart, and I cried tears of joy again.

To make good on my promise to let go of Rebecca and give her back to God, I sent her an email. In it I shared how I had come to realize what a great blessing and gift she was, how much I appreciated her many sacrifices through the years, and how I was following her example and committing my life to following Jesus and submitting in all of my ways.

"I've learned that faith requires submission and trusting God," I wrote with tears in my eyes, "So this is me submitting and letting you go. Thank you for giving so much of your heart. I'm truly sorry I didn't give more of mine. Love always, Mark."

Then I hovered over the SEND button with the mouse pointer... pressed the mouse button down... held it for a few seconds as the past 14 tumultuous years of love and pain rapidly flashed through my mind... and <u>let go</u>. And when I did, I prayed for the first time that Rebecca would never come home again... unless she first went to Jesus.

Rebecca: Mark's email caught me by surprise, just as I had begun feeling like I was coming down with the flu. I didn't know what was more shocking: his new gratitude and kindness, or that he had apparently been born again. Either way, it made me very emotional, and I went to sleep that night feeling torn and unsettled.

Mark: Immediately after I sent the email, I began experiencing even greater peace of mind and rest of heart. My anxiety was nearly gone, and I felt exponentially more hopeful and optimistic than I had in years. And it wasn't hope for our marriage to be restored; it was hope in God that He was making a good way for me, even if I couldn't see it.

Peace Patio

That night I dreamt of having a small patio in the corner of my backyard and envisioned myself laying on a bench there in perfect peace. I shared the dream with my kids, and they said we should build it. We named it "Peace Patio," and agreed it would be a place to sit and *be still*, read the Bible, play their guitars, listen, and get to know the Lord's voice.

With a pile of bricks from Home Depot and a few shovels we cleared a space in the ground and laid the foundation together, stone by stone. As we worked together, they told me about the many things they had learned about following Jesus, and I was astonished by their knowledge. I flashed back to how upset I had been that Rebecca was taking them to church and was humbled again. I asked God to forgive me.

Throughout the day, I felt increasingly uplifted and hopeful about the future and at some point, miraculously started believing our marriage was going to be restored. I don't even remember how it occurred to me. I just remember thinking, "God is going to make this happen." It was a deeply-rooted intuition I never experienced before. Someone would tell me later, "That was the intuition of faith."

Then I started talking to God—not just with single verses, but with multiple verses that formed longer prayers. "God you are all powerful, if you are for me no one can be against me, I can do all things through Christ who strengthens me, and I *know* you will make a way even though I can't see a way right now. I trust you God," I prayed. I wasn't 100% sure of those things yet, but I was 100% sure it felt right, and every time I did it, I felt more worry and anxiety fall away.

In the afternoon, after teaching the Hanon piano exercises to my son, I was delighted to see my daughter sitting on the Peace Patio bench playing her guitar and singing. I walked out, sat next to her, and listened intently to her beautiful voice and music. She was singing a song about the power of faith.

She asked how I was doing. I said, "I'm finally at peace because I've put all my hope in God, and I'm OK with whatever He decides. I'm sorry there has been so much turmoil in our lives for so long, but I didn't understand what it meant to be a *real man* after God's own heart until recently. Now I'm going to live for God and for love, and starting today I want to build a better relationship with you and your brother and be the dad God has called me to be."

She smiled and said, "Dad, I love you," and hugged me tightly.

As we embraced, I prayed to God with all of my heart our family could be healed and thanked Him for every blessing. I thanked Him for my life, my children, my countless other blessings, and most of all my faith. For it was through the gift and lens of faith that I could finally *see* the good in my life and all around me, especially the love in my arms at that very moment.

When I went back inside and logged onto my computer, there was an amazing Scripture in my email from a "Daily Bible Verse" service I had subscribed to. To this day it is one I look to daily for hope.

God says, "See, I am doing a new thing! Now it springs up; do you not perceive it? I am making a way in the wilderness and streams in the wasteland." -Isaiah 43:19 (NIV)

I cried tears of joy because I could finally *perceive* it. I didn't know exactly what it was yet, but I finally believed God was with me, and He was doing something wonderful, something good, and harm would not come to me.

In the evening, Mateo sent me another Scripture reminding me that everything was going to be OK, even if the divorce was finalized in court later that week. It read:

"For I know the plans I have for you," declares the LORD, "plans to prosper you and not to harm you, plans to give you hope and a future." -Jeremiah 29:11 (NIV)

That night I slept soundly because I had come to know that God would be with me and my mind was finally at rest. I had truly begun to believe His power was real, and I was no longer afraid of the future—even if it was unknown.

Moreover, I no longer had the desire to change Rebecca's mind or heart. I had come to believe that *only Jesus* could do that. I had finally found the peace and freedom I had set out for... at the foot of the Cross.

Breaking Impossible

With only two days remaining until our official divorce date, I awoke Monday morning feeling a great sense of anticipation, as though something spectacular was about to happen.

Recharged with new purpose and feeling gratitude for every gift God had given me, I stopped by the grocery store before work and was moved to greet everyone I encountered with a smile and a kind word. I praised God constantly because He had finally lifted me out of that dark, sunken place I had been in for so long. Then the impossible happened.

Soon after starting my work day, our daughter messaged me and said she was worried about Rebecca because she had been very sick and was bedridden. Out of concern I called Rebecca and asked if there was anything I could do to help.

Her response was like a cold slap in the face. "Yes, you can help... by leaving me alone."

Ouch. I was deeply saddened by how bitter and distant she had become. Then suddenly from somewhere deep in my soul I gently asked her a question I had never conceived before:

"Why is your heart so hard??"

The second those words left my mouth I braced for another hailstorm of accusations, but to my astonishment there was only silence. Then, after a long pause, she started crying and spoke words that still bring tears to my eyes as I write them:

"I can't fight it anymore. This past weekend I got sick and very weak, but on Sunday I still felt a huge tug on my heart to go to church. I was so weak I sat in the back and didn't even have the energy to sing worship songs. The sermon was all about submission... how we have to submit to God and trust Him in *all* of our ways, not just the ones that are comfortable... and..."

"And what?" I urged her on.

"And I just broke down in tears because I realized God had been trying to get me to submit and trust Him with saving our marriage, but I had refused because I was too angry and too afraid of getting hurt again..."

Deeply touched by her honesty, I replied, "I see."

Rebecca: I could tell by Mark's empathetic tone that something had changed. I think that was the first time he was actively listening rather than trying to steer the conversation (and my heart). For once I felt I could be vulnerable without fear of being controlled. So I took a leap of faith and revealed the rest of my heart.

Then I said, "So after church I went home and asked God to remove the pride walls from my heart and show me the way He wanted me to walk because I just couldn't see any way possible... and then... this morning when you asked why my heart was so hard... I could finally see the way..."

Mark: "What way is that?" I asked, still not having any idea where she was going.

She was so choked up she could barely get the words out. "I see the way is Jesus... and if we submit to Him and each other we can forgive, heal, and finally have a happy marriage like couples I have met at my church."

It was a miracle. *"Really? Are you serious?"* I asked in disbelief, my heart skipping beats. "I don't know what to say. *Are you sure?"*

"No," I'm not sure," she said firmly. "But I'm sure this is God's will, and I'm willing to trust Him and follow it... if you are."

"I am!" I said joyfully. "As I said in my text to you, I've learned *all things* are possible if Jesus is our Lord and Savior." I couldn't believe the words coming out of my heart. But the words she said next were even more unbelievable.

"So, how about we meet with your counselor friend and see how it goes?" she asked.

"Mateo? You want to meet with Mateo? Yes! That would be amazing! But you're sick right now, so..."

"I'm actually feeling better and this is more important," she said.

Unlocked

At that, we quickly ended the call and I dialed Mateo immediately. "You'll never guess what happened, my brother!" I said excitedly.

"What's up my brother?" he laughed.

"It's a miracle. Rebecca said she went to church and heard about submitting to God and recommitted her life to Jesus, and she thinks our marriage can work if we follow His way together and—she says she wants to meet with you!"

"Well praise the Lord!" he roared. "You both need to come down to my studio NOW!" I was shocked he was ready to meet at that moment.

I called Rebecca back and amazingly she said she'd be right over. I then called my boss and told him a miracle had occurred, and I needed to go see a marriage counselor with my wife. I will never forget his words. "Congrats my friend, that's wonderful news, take all the time you need, and let me know how it goes." Another miracle.

After those calls, I stood in my kitchen staring at the phone in shock. I couldn't believe what was happening. I remember thinking, *Either I'm dreaming, or I'm right now witnessing mountains move by grace and faith.*

A short while later I heard a car door slam and jogged to the front window to look out. What a sight to behold. There was Rebecca exiting her car, walking up my driveway to go to Mateo's studio with me. I could have sworn the light outside grew brighter with every step she took.

It was hard to fathom only a few weeks ago I stood in that same exact spot looking out the window in awe of my neighbor Matt's devotion, questioning why God would convict me with such a powerful vision of love and harmony if Rebecca was never coming back. My heart overflowed with gratitude and hope as I unlocked the deadbolt and opened the door to a new life...

Reflections

Our only reflection here is complete, thunderstruck awe of God's power, and endless gratitude for His mercy and grace. #NOTW

The *Last* Breakup

18: Divine Reconciliation

"And I will give them one heart, and a new spirit I will put within them. I will remove the heart of stone from their flesh and give them a heart of flesh." Ezekiel 11:19 (ESV)

"He made the storm be still, and the waves of the sea were hushed. Then they were glad that the waters were quiet, and he brought them to their desired haven." -Psalms 107:29 (ESV)

Mark: When I opened the front door to let Rebecca in, we immediately embraced without a word. Then my heart leapt for joy when we locked eyes briefly, and I saw in hers a spark of innocence and joyful hope that I couldn't recall ever seeing before.

Rebecca: That was the most unguarded and giving hug I ever felt from Mark. As we prepared to leave for Mateo's studio, I felt great hope that with God and a Christian counselor's help we might finally be able to leave our messy past behind and have a loving marriage and friendship like the ones I encountered at church. That hope overshadowed my doubts and fears—at least for the moment.

Touchdown

Mark: Neither of us recall what we talked about on the drive to Mateo's studio, but we remember our arrival like it was yesterday. He met us in the parking lot, smiling ear to ear, holding his arms above his head victoriously as if we had just scored a game winning touchdown.

Not surprisingly, he jogged up to Rebecca like he had known her his whole life and hugged her the same way he hugged me the first time we met in the lobby of Chili's. If I didn't know better, I would have thought they were best friends. I saw the tears in Rebecca's eyes and knew something special, something not of this world, was happening.

Rebecca: I felt the same love I had been feeling ever since I started going to church, and it was the welcoming and accepting friendship of a grace-filled heart.

Mark: Then he hugged me and whispered in my ear, "God is so good. I *told* you *all things* were possible!" I cried tears of joy on his shoulder.

As we embraced it struck me that I no longer felt indifferent or awkward from his affection, but rather a deep bond of brotherly love. I think it was in that embrace I came to believe if the love of God could unite two completely different men from completely different worlds together in perfect harmony, it could do the same—and even more—for Rebecca and me. I prayed silently again, *I believe Lord, help my unbelief.*

Inside the studio, Rebecca and I sat in chairs next to each other, and Mateo bowed his head and prayed. "Holy Father we are gathered together here today for one reason and that is because you brought us here. Only *you* have the power to unite the hearts of a man and woman together in harmony, only *you* have the power to salvage an unsalvageable marriage, and only *you* deserve all the honor, praise, and glory.

"We ask that you bless us with supernatural ability to hear the truth in our hearts, so the Holy Spirit of Truth and love can lead us to understanding, healing, and restoration. In Jesus name, amen."

Rebecca: As Mateo prayed, I felt even more powerful love and belonging in my heart than when I first attended Grace Heart church. It was God's love, and I could see how it was bringing everything and everyone together in perfect harmony. I knew at that moment God was there with us, and it was *safe* to open my heart.

Then I was moved to do something that I never fathomed I could ever do again: I reached over and held Mark's hand.

Mark: Feeling Rebecca's touch sent shockwaves of joy and hope through me. Between that and Mateo's prayer, whatever pride remained in my heart was crushed into a fine powder, and I too felt divine reassurance that it was safe to be fully truthful.

We didn't realize it until we sat down to write this book, but it was the first time that neither of us actually *feared* what the other would say. We've learned that was because we were submitted, and the Holy Spirit of truth and love had entered our hearts and given us the faith and courage to speak the truth in love to each other.

The Heart of the Matter

Following his prayer Mateo leaned toward us with a solemn expression and asked, "I need to ask you one question. Do you believe that God can and will heal your hearts and save your marriage?"

When we said we did, he smiled joyfully and declared, "Well praise the Lord because that's the most important faith step you will ever take together. I need to tell you I believe it too, and I also believe God is going to give you a powerful message from your mess, and a powerful testimony from your tests, and your marriage will become a great ministry for His glory one day.

Rebecca: That was the most inspiring vision I ever heard, yet it was so far beyond anything I ever dreamed possible it was hard to believe. We still had so much pain, baggage, dirty laundry, and drama in our past to get over, it just seemed inconceivable. Old unbelief dies hard.

Then he announced, "OK, now I'd like you to share your testimonies from your heart about how you came to believe God can heal your marriage. *The stage is yours."*

Six months earlier I couldn't have even fathomed opening my heart for any reason, let alone to share my belief that God could save our marriage. But by the grace of God I had developed unshakable confidence to speak freely and fearlessly, and it was because I had come to believe that God's love never fails, and in His love, I couldn't fail either.

Then I shared how my road to happiness and freedom led to the truth about the ways we hurt each other in our marriage... and how my heart wounds ran deeper than just our marriage and I needed Jesus to heal them... and finally... the sobering realization that the root cause of our dysfunction and division was not our irreconcilable differences, but that our souls had not been reconciled with

God. And without God's love and forgiveness through Jesus, we couldn't forgive and love each other.

Mark: It was a miracle. I was astonished by how God—it had to be God—brought Rebecca and I to the same essential truths, through totally different circumstances and people, while we were apart. Captivated and humbled by her beautiful testimony of miraculous grace, all I could think to say was, "Amen." And I realized Mateo's prophesy that God had been working on our hearts had come to pass.

After sharing his amazement over God's power to soften Rebecca's heart and bring her to the truth, Mateo said, "OK Mr. Mark, the stage is yours."

I recalled how closed off and shaky I was when he first said those same words the day we met. I was so weirded out by his teachings about playing from my heart and making connections with people I couldn't even meet with him again. Yet here I was, months later, broken, humbled, and awakened, moved by God to testify from my heart and make a connection with Rebecca. It hit me that God's love was completing the circle of giving.

I then let go and shared how Rebecca's honesty about her feelings made me confront the truth about myself... how all the things I relied on and hoped in shifted under my feet and I fell... how God finally opened my eyes to see my heart was missing from my marriage because it was divided from Him and hardened due to my unbelief... and how I finally came to see and accept that despite my religious background I was faithless and didn't know

God… and the reason was because I had never repented and given my life to Jesus.

Upon the conclusion of our testimonies Rebecca and I were deeply moved to apologize to each other again. Then we cried, embraced, and thanked God for each other. When I looked over at Mateo he was crying too and whispered, "Praise God, praise God, thank you Jesus, this is a divine reconciliation."

Gifts

When we regrouped Mateo said he had never witnessed such a miraculous restoration before and was in complete awe that God had reconciled us through Jesus before we even got to his studio. He reiterated that God had amazing plans for us, and he couldn't wait to see them unfold.

"I'm amazed because your testimonies speak the Biblical truth," he said. "I'm praising God because I know He is present and divinely restoring you. Now if you keep submitting, learning, and exercising faith, God is going to do amazing things with your lives and marriage. Do you believe that?" We said we did.

"Good!" he exclaimed. "Now, before you go, we need to talk about a few fundamentals. First, your hearts are gifts from God, and He wants you to give your hearts and other gifts to Him, each other, your kids, and others. In that order. The Bible says. 'As each has received a gift, use it to serve one another, as good stewards of God's varied grace.' So treat each other's hearts as precious gifts." -1 Peter 4:10 (ESV)

Suddenly everything he taught me in my first piano lesson about "sharing your gift and reaching your higher purpose" made perfect sense.

Rebecca: He also taught us our battle was not against flesh but evil spirits, that there was a spiritual war being waged for our souls and marriage, and the only way we could achieve victory was surrendering daily to Jesus so we could put on the armor of God together. He said that meant putting God *first*, and how if we weren't willing to do that, we ran the risk of failing again. (Ephesians 6:10-17)

"The only way you will succeed," he counseled us, "is if you live for God and not each other, and with strength from Jesus work together *as a team* to protect your marriage as you would a precious jewel, never allowing anyone to come between you. You have to remember your heart is where your treasure is. If God is not your treasure, your heart will not be in your marriage." (Matthew 6:21)

I had been hearing it for months, but for some reason it didn't sink in until Mateo said it: the most important treasure in life was not marriage or even family, it was the gift of salvation and the love of God that came through surrender; and only a life lived through the vine of Jesus Christ *together* could produce the loving and harmonious fruits of marriage that both of us desired.

Mark: He taught us many other things, but none with so much zeal as he taught the non-negotiable necessity of learning God's word and obeying it. He said in order to grow in love and become closer to God and each other, our hearts had to be sanctified (purified, made Holy), and the only way that could happen was if we heard the word of God and the Holy Spirit testified and illuminated it in our hearts. (John 17:17).

"Man cannot live on bread alone, but by every word that proceedeth out of the mouth of God," he said. "The Word of God must reign supreme in your lives, because it is truth, and through submission the Holy Spirit will give you the love, wisdom, faith, and strength your marriage needs to thrive and grow." (Matthew 4:4)

It was a lot to digest, but we got the most important part: we needed to learn the voice of Truth, the Word of God, and live by it and no other.

At the end of the session, he pointed to one of his pianos and said if we worshiped Christ together as our Lord and Savior, the Holy Spirit would unite our hearts together just like the unique keys of the piano, and we would produce harmonious music that pleased God, ourselves, and others.

Rebecca: Out in the parking lot of his studio, he embraced us in a big group bear hug and made us promise to continue counseling with him so he could "scaffold" us until we were strong enough to become dependent on God. He also reminded us that if we fixed our eyes on God, we would be kept in perfect peace. (Isaiah 26:3).

Then he reiterated his prediction. "One day your marriage is going to become a ministry and testimony, and Mark will write a book about it." His optimism was unlike anything we had ever heard... though we couldn't yet imagine the marriage he envisioned for us.

First Steps

Mark: When Rebecca and I got in the car we cried again. Neither of us ever felt so loved, worthy, and hopeful before. And while we were happy for Mateo and our reunion, the joy that filled our eyes with tears came from the all-powerful, redemptive love of God that was overflowing out of our hearts. Through surrender to Jesus we had come to know the love of God,

After we caught our breath I turned to Rebecca and asked, "Soooo, does this mean the divorce party's off?"

She wittily jabbed back, "Yes. Is that your way of asking me to marry you again?" We laughed and embraced again, and when our cheeks touched our tears of joy became one.

Rebecca: Of course I still had many unhealed wounds and fears we would fail again. On top of that, I was sad to give up my condo and even sadder to have to disconnect from the amazing people I had met.

But overshadowing my sadness was my firm belief that God wanted Mark and I together and that we would heal in time if we stayed connected to Him. I truly believed Mark and I had been divinely reconciled—not just by band-aids, empty promises, and good intentions (as in the past), but by the healing blood of Jesus, and God's inseparable love.

Mark and Rebecca: As we drove *home*, we thanked God for his mercy and grace and marveled at His power to soften our hearts and bring us into loving harmony together in Mateo's "Music for the Heart Strings" studio. And upon realizing God had miraculously merged our separate roads in search of fulfillment back together at the foot of the Cross of Christ, we knew we had witnessed our very *last break up.*

Reflections

We are witnesses to the power of grace through faith to move mountains of baggage, pains, wounds, and closed hearts to make a way in the wilderness for healing and harmony.

Looking back, we are in awe of the fact that by the time we got to Mateo's studio that day we had already been saved and reconciled. We had come to know the truth, and we were already made free to love and heal by the time we entered his door. Notably, he was just as stunned by God's grace and power as we were.

For 14 years we tried every way under the sun to fix our marriage and failed miserably again and again and again... to the brink of insanity. The common denominator between all those failures is that we were trying to impose our wills and ideas of love on each other, rather than submitting to Jesus and the will of God to receive His beautiful and harmonizing love (which we couldn't do because the truth had not been welcome in our home).

The absence of the truth in our hearts and lives shackled us to sin, fears, pride, and the need to control each other, which suffocated God's unfailing love and never allowed it to be our master. Instead we were mastered by fear and deception, sin, and unable to submit to God and each other. When we finally surrendered, let go, and put our faith and love in Jesus, the Holy Spirit of

God's grace and truth entered our hearts and finally *freed us* to love, listen, learn, forgive, and begin healing.

"So if the Son sets you free, you shall be free indeed."
-John 8:36 (NKJV)

Only the love of God through Christ can move people from all walks of life to serve His purposes and share their gifts so generously and completely for the good of others as Mateo, Sarah, and others did for us.

Only the love of God through Christ can melt down walls of irreconcilable pride, fear, resentment, and even hatred, and reconcile two shattered hearts together as one spiritual flesh in Christ.

Only the love of God in Jesus Christ can do these things. We are witnesses.

"And above all these put on love, which binds everything together in perfect harmony. And let the peace of Christ rule in your hearts, to which you were indeed called in one body.," -Colossians 3:14 (ESV)

"For by grace you have been saved through faith. And this is not your own doing; it is the gift of God, not a result of works, so that no one may boast." -Ephesians 2:8 (ESV)

The *Last* Breakup

19: Walk This Way

"And this is love: that we walk in obedience to his commands. As you have heard from the beginning, his command is that you walk in love." -2 John 1:6 (NIV)

"For where your treasure is, there your heart will be also." -Matthew 6:21 (NIV)

Redemption by Grace

Mark: Convinced that God wanted us together, and that with devoted faith we could heal, build a new relationship in Christ, and have an amazing marriage like those we had witnessed while we were apart, we took a massive leap of faith and drove to the courthouse to cancel our divorce. It was the very last day of the six-month waiting period.

The clerk who processed our cancellation request said she had never seen a divorce withdrawn on the day before the dissolution date. We briefly shared our story and testified that with God all things are possible.

She smiled and replied, "Amen! I'm a believer!" It was the first of many testimonies we would share together. We realized Mateo's prediction had come to pass: God had made a message from our mess, and a testimony from our tests.

As we signed the final documents, I looked at our fingers and marveled at the sight of our wedding rings around them again. When the clerk stamped the papers and bid us good luck, I felt like we had just redeemed that winning lotto ticket. And I marveled again at God's power to redeem what I once fervently believed was a totally irredeemable marriage.

Before departing, we were moved to take a short rest under a sprawling oak tree in the courtyard outside and pray. We prayed for God's love, faith, healing, and wisdom for us and our children. We prayed for the endurance to follow Jesus all the days of our lives. We thanked God for every blessing and for every friend who led us to the light of truth.

And though it felt unfamiliar and even a little awkward to submit to God and pray together for the first time, it felt good and pure and profoundly liberating to put our hope in God rather than ourselves and each other.

Rebecca: When we got home, I called Sarah and told her the news of our reconciliation. She jumped for joy and said, "Thank you Jesus." I can't even begin to express how much hope and courage she gave me that day. Her love and encouragement were food for my soul, especially since so many of our friends and family thought we were out of our minds for canceling our divorce. I'm certain she was an angel sent by God.

Mark: I called several people also. One was Aaron. Upon hearing the news, he exalted, "Praise Jesus. Praise Jesus. I'm happy for you my friend. Now keep turning to God and get ready for the tests." I had to laugh because no matter what I told him he always had something to add. I had no idea what he was talking about, and figured he was just being... Aaron. Old pride dies hard.

The Suitcase

Mark: Unfortunately, we got so busy with the transition we didn't get around to meeting with Mateo again—for piano or marriage lessons. We were so overjoyed by our miraculous reconciliation that we fell into the "DIY" trap of thinking we could find our way on our own. We figured if we attended church regularly, put our relationship first, and prayed a lot all would be well with our souls. But nope.

One day out of the clear blue sky of our new life together, a series of "when-it-rains-it-pours" life storms rolled in, and suddenly we found ourselves sinking again. Then came conflicts, emotions, old accusations, and division. I grew weary, Rebecca began to lose heart, and we even feared our reconciliation was a mistake. Finally, I let go again and sent Mateo an SOS text saying, "We're in trouble. Help."

Mark and Rebecca: The next day we were back in his studio again, hugging, praying, hearing God's word, learning, testifying, rejoicing, crying, and miraculously rekindling the spirit of faith, love, and hope we encountered together the first time we met with him. Once again, by the grace of God, we had humbly surrendered, and once again God had exalted us.

When we were in the final stages of writing this book, we shared this part of our testimony with a friend. She responded, "Wow! I want to know Mateo's secret!" We answered her the same way the gardeners answered me. "Jesus. He's a disciple and knows the word of God, and the word of God has resurrection POWER to save and heal surrendered hearts."

And that is exactly what he reiterated we needed to do to get back on track and protect our marriage from failure.

That day he retaught us one of the most important "fundamentals" we've learned as Christians and husband and wife. We heard it previously, but it didn't truly *sink in* until that day, when our hearts were wide open again, and we were actively listening and seeking truth as students. The lesson was derived from the word of God in the book of Ephesians:

"For our struggle is not against flesh and blood, but against the rulers, against the authorities, against the powers of this dark world and against the spiritual forces of evil in the heavenly realms." -Ephesians 6:12 (NIV)

Mateo said we were in the midst of a spiritual war being waged against God, His children, and everything good, especially love and marriage. This war, he said, was being waged by the ruler of this world, the evil one, the prince of lies and darkness, the author of fear and confusion, the arch enemy of God, the father of sin who conquers by deception and division, named Satan.

He explained only Jesus has dominion over Satan, so therefore we must abide by faith in Jesus to conquer the spirit of evil that was trying to tear us from God's love and each other. He said if we didn't abide faithfully in Jesus, we would be vulnerable to Satan's complex schemes and deceptions and enticed and dragged away from God—and each other—again.

"When you fall away from God," he counseled us, "you are deprived of His love and truth, and then you start listening to other voices, including your own, especially your emotions. Never trust your emotions as the truth. Only the Bible is the truth.

"If you disobey God and start following any other voice than the voice of the Holy Spirit in your heart, you will doubt, doubt, doubt. And as James says in the Bible you will become 'double-minded and unstable in all of your ways.' Then you will lose heart, lose hope, and ultimately, much to the delight of Satan, you will lose your way again.

"Do you know how Jesus overcame Satan when Satan tried to deceive Him?" We didn't. "He told him the *truth* with Scripture. When Satan offered him all the kingdoms of the world if Jesus would worship Him, Jesus said, "Away from me, Satan! For it is written: 'Worship the Lord your God and serve him only. Then the devil left him, and angels came and attended him.'" -Matthew 4:8 (NIV)

He reiterated the fundamental truth we had both learned before but had somehow forgotten already: the only way to remain one with God in love, and protected against the enemy's lies and temptations was to obey God's commands and stay rooted in the immovable and immutable <u>truth</u> of God's word.

"Be strong in the Lord and in the power of his might. Put on the whole armor of God, that you may be able to stand against the wiles of the devil." -Ephesians 6:10 (NKJV)

"In order to do that," he counseled, "You must put *Jesus first*, even before each other and your marriage, and love and trust Him and His word more than you love and trust each other. You can't have any other Gods before you—not even your marriage. You must walk His way and no other."

Mark: When I asked him how to put Jesus first, he lit up and pointed to a piano nearby. "Same way I taught you how to learn jazz piano. You become an obedient-hearted *student*—a student of Jesus Christ called a *disciple*."

He then walked to the other side of his study, grabbed the huge, out-of-place suitcase that was in the corner, dragged it over, opened it, dumped it on the floor, and to our amazement out came at least 50 Bibles and Bible-based books on every topic imaginable.

We all had a good laugh, and I finally realized what he meant when he said at the end of my first meeting with him, "Every great master is first a great student."

Mark and Rebecca: As he put the books back in the suitcase he said, "You must invite the Holy Spirit into your home and heart daily. Read and hear God's word in a peaceful place alone and at church with fellow believers. Allow the Holy Spirit of Truth to illuminate God's word so your heart can be made pure and resistant to the enemy's temptations. The Holy Spirit's testimony is supreme above all others.

"Learn the fundamental truths and practice them diligently in your life like the Hanon exercises I gave you. You will be strengthening your faith, so you don't doubt. And you will learn to hear God's voice, follow it, and play in time with Him so you can not only stand firm together in love and truth, but actually make beautiful music for God and others.

"When you put Jesus first and pick up your cross and follow Him daily, you will be blessed with the supernatural power to discern between good and evil, truth and deception, see through the enemy's lies, and stay on the straight and narrow road of love and truth, rather than be enticed and dragged into darkness by sin, apart from God and each other.

"When you put Jesus first, you will no longer be mastered by emotions, fears, anger and false teachings that drive you apart. Instead you will be mastered by truth and grace and ascend to the marital love and harmony God designed you for. Then and only then will you *know the way*, even through life's dark valleys and torrential storms."

"Whether you turn to the right or to the left, your ears will hear a voice behind you, saying, "This is the way; walk in it." -Isaiah 30:21 (NIV)

He continued, "Jesus is the way, the truth, and the life, and only living by His example will God bless you with the power of the Spirit to sanctify your hearts, fully heal your past, and bless you with the fruits of the spirit in Galatians 5:22 that your marriage requires to live and thrive for God's glory.

"Jesus is the only way. There is no other way to victory. *The wages of sin is death,* death of soul, death of love, death of spirit, death of marriage, and Jesus is the only one who has overcome sin and death. You either walk the way of spirit, grace, and truth as He did, or you will fall away." (Romans 6:23; John 1:14)

By the time we left his studio that day, we were absolutely certain Christian discipleship, the way of grace and truth, the way of love, the way of Jesus, was the only way we wanted to walk going forward. And from that day forward we began to seek...

Spiritual Transformation by Truth

Due to our pride and aversion to study and learning, it didn't happen overnight, but gradually we began to submit our hearts to God through Jesus daily and look to His word as our guiding light truth and treasure. In doing so we began to shift our focus from the material to the spiritual; and by that, I mean we focused on being conformed to the image of Christ, in heart, mind, and spirit. This became our daily prayer, and one we still pray all the time:

"Create in me a clean heart, O God, and renew a right spirit within me." -Psalm 51:10 (ESV)

Miraculously, we found the more we submitted to God, learned His word and obeyed it, the more we came to know His love, and the more we desired to submit and love each other (rather than endlessly strive to please each other).

It has only been through submission to God that our "irreconcilable differences" have become our strengths, and we have gained the power and endurance to walk the way of Christ. And the way of Christ is the way of love, as expressed in 1 Corinthians 13 that we hear at so many weddings:

"Love is patient, love is kind. It does not envy, it does not boast, it is not proud. It does not dishonor others, it is not self-seeking, it is not easily angered, it keeps no record of wrongs. Love does not delight in evil but rejoices with the truth. It always protects, always trusts, always hopes, always perseveres." -1 Corinthians 13 (NIV)

And we're not just talking about love for each other; we're talking about love for our neighbors.

Of course that's not to imply we have mastered it. Not even close. We need to "stay in the word of Truth" every day to walk the way of love and truth, especially when it comes to bearing with each other with a heart of mercy and grace, which is critical to the health of all relationships, especially marriage.

We have so much more to say about the ongoing spiritual transformation of our hearts and minds; but the main point we want to make now is that while we still face storms of trial and tribulation, they no longer tear us apart. Rather, through mutual surrender to Christ as our one and only Lord and Savior, our trials have only strengthened us and brought us closer to God and each other.

Now, rather than separating every time a storm comes, rather than going to various people and going out on various limbs for shelter, rather than dodging the truth because it's uncomfortable, we go to Jesus, and the Holy Spirit gives us the power to bear with each other, tell the truth to each other in love, and be still and wait on the Lord to deliver us.

Now, Miraculously, every time we find ourselves at odds with each other, God reconciles us again... and again… and again. Our marriage pattern is no longer failure, but victory.

Walking the way of Christ and experiencing God's healing and restorative love, in 2008 we were moved to rewrite our wedding vows. They included a vow to learn the word of God so we could come to know His voice of truth, live by it, and be conformed to the image of Jesus, as God wills. A few months later we renewed our wedding vows in front of all of our friends and family and declared our commitment to follow Jesus together.

Shortly thereafter we submitted official "letters of resignation" to each other, in which we resigned from being each other's saviors and everythings and agreed to worship Jesus as our only Lord and Savior.

From that day forward, we began experiencing a new level of freedom in our marriage to simply be friends in Christ that we had never known before. It is that spirit of friendship in Christ that bonds us in love and harmony to this day.

As we continued to seek truth and grow spiritually in Christ together, our marriage blossomed. From the spirit of truth came beautiful spiritual fruits of love so abundant that we overflowed with gratitude for God's grace and became deeply compelled to love, serve, and testify to others.

And while we still have doubts and fears, and stumble like everyone else, we continue to seek the *way of love and truth*. In accordance with Jesus' commandment in Matthew 11:28, we try to put all our hope in God alone and remember to go to Him before anyone else. And that is why we are still together, and deeply in love.

Last Word

We now approach life as a learning journey of God's word and will so we can answer Christ's commands to love God and neighbor as ourselves and be the "lights" we have been called to be. As for church, we finally found one we believe ministers the true word of God, and being part of the body of Christ is an important part of our walk.

In that spirit, we strive to be disciples of Christ and view our home as a "greenhouse of His love and truth." Consequently, we are increasingly finding that His grace is fully sufficient for us, and His power is made perfect in our weakness.

On that grace note, the last word we want to leave you with is SURRENDER. Surrender of what? Surrender of our whole hearts to Jesus so God's love—His spirit of truth, mercy, and grace—can reach its full measure in us.

"My child, give me your heart, and let your eyes observe my ways." Proverbs 23:26 (ESV)

It was through surrender that we were blessed with new life, true love, healing, and hope just when all hoped seemed lost. It was through surrender that our souls and marriage were saved. It is through daily surrender that we are able to endure by faith and live together harmoniously in God's love.

And it is only through surrender that we were able to bear witness to the Truth (dirty laundry and all) of God's saving grace through Jesus Christ in this book for the glory of God, and bear with each other for the 22 months it took to write this book.

We leave you with this truth in love for the glory of God: Surrender your heart to God, and the love, peace, and fulfillment your heart desires will follow. We are witnesses. We pray that you may be witnesses also. Amen.

"But as for me in my house, we will serve the LORD."
-Joshua 24:15 (ESV)

"Therefore, what God has brought together, let man not separate." -Mark 10:9 (NKJV)

Epilogue

After their divine reconciliation in 2007, Mark and Rebecca discovered new love in Christ and never broke up again. In 2019, they celebrated their 26th wedding anniversary. They spend their spare time together reading the word, serving, witnessing, cooking, hiking, and listening to long playlists of their favorite music.

Mark began ministering the truth in love to his dad shortly after his conversion. Seven years later his dad repented and believed in Jesus before he passed away.

In 2012 Rebecca was moved to pursue her passion for photography. A year later, her and Mark opened a wedding photography business and have shot over 100 weddings together to date. When people ask them the secret to their harmonious marriage and working relationship, they always respond, "Jesus."

From time to time Mateo checks in to see how Mark and Rebecca are doing and encourages them to keep learning the word and testifying about God's greatness.

By the grace of God, Mark retired from being a selfaholic, workaholic, self-sufficient warrior, smoker, competitive fitness addict, drinker, and scoffer, and now dedicates his life to sharing the good news of the Gospel and serving the kingdom of God.

Mark finally learned to play the Hanon exercises on the piano but hasn't progressed beyond them... yet...

A: Divine Encouragement

The following Scriptures spoke the most to our hearts as we wrote this book. We pray they are a great a blessing to you as they have been for us. And we pray when you are faced with uncertainty and your faith is being tested, you hear God's voice of truth in these words, and it guides you to the Light.

Please note: All scriptures in this section taken from the Holy Bible: New International Version. See Appendix C for copyright information.

—

"The Son is the image of the invisible God, the firstborn over all creation. For in him all things were created: things in heaven and on earth, visible and invisible, whether thrones or powers or rulers or authorities; all things have been created through him and for him. He is before all things, and in him all things hold together. And he is the head of the body, the church; he is the beginning and the firstborn from among the dead, so that in everything he might have the supremacy. For God was pleased to have all his fullness dwell in him, and through him to reconcile to himself all things, whether things on earth or things in heaven, by making peace through his blood, shed on the cross.

"Once you were alienated from God and were enemies in your minds because of your evil behavior. But now he has reconciled you by Christ's physical body through death to present you holy in his sight, without blemish and free from accusation— if you continue in your faith, established and firm, and do not move from the hope held out in the gospel. This is the gospel that you heard and that has been proclaimed to every creature under heaven, and of which I, Paul, have become a servant." -Colossians 1:21

—

"Follow the way of love." -1 Corinthians 14

—

"This is love: not that we loved God, but that he loved us and sent his Son as an atoning sacrifice for our sins... since God so loved us, we also ought to love one another. No one has ever seen God; but if we love one another, God lives in us and his love is made complete in us... This is how we know that we live in him and he in us: He has given us of his Spirit... God is love. Whoever lives in love lives in God, and God in them." -1 John 4:10-16

—

"I kneel before the Father, from whom every family in heaven and on earth derives its name. I pray that out of his glorious riches he may strengthen you with power through his Spirit in your inner being, so that Christ may dwell in your hearts through faith. And I pray that you, being rooted and established in love, may have power, together with all the Lord's holy people, to grasp how wide and long and high and deep is the love of Christ, and to know this love that surpasses knowledge—that you may be filled to the measure of all the fullness of God." -Ephesians 3:14

—

"For this very reason, make every effort to add to your faith goodness; and to goodness, knowledge; and to knowledge, self-control; and to self-control, perseverance; and to perseverance, godliness; and to godliness, mutual affection; and to mutual affection, love. For if you possess these qualities in increasing measure, they will keep you from being ineffective and unproductive in your knowledge of our Lord Jesus Christ. But whoever does not have them is nearsighted and blind, forgetting that they have been cleansed from their past sins." -2 Peter 1:5

—

"I pray that out of his glorious riches he may strengthen you with power through his Spirit in your inner being, so that Christ may dwell in your hearts through faith. And I pray that you, being rooted and established in love, may have power, together with all the Lord's holy people, to grasp how wide and long and high and deep is the love of Christ, and to know this love that surpasses knowledge—that you may be filled to the measure of all the fullness of God." -Ephesians 3:16

—

"I have been crucified with Christ and I no longer live, but Christ lives in me. The life I now live in the body, I live by faith in the Son of God, who loved me and gave himself for me." -Galatians 2:20

—

"But those who hope in the LORD will renew their strength. They will soar on wings like eagles; they will run and not grow weary, they will walk and not be faint." -Isaiah 40:31

—

"Do not store up for yourselves treasures on earth, where moths and vermin destroy, and where thieves break in and steal. But store up for yourselves treasures in heaven, where moths and vermin do not destroy, and where thieves do not break in and steal. For where your treasure is, there your heart (and marriage) will be also." -Matthew 6:19

—

"Ask, and it will be given to you; seek, and you will find; knock, and it will be opened to you. -Matthew 7:7

—

"Jesus said, My peace I leave with you; my peace I give to you. Not as the world gives do I give to you. Let not your hearts be troubled, neither let them be afraid." -John 14:27

—

"Sanctify them by the truth; your word is truth." -John 17:17

—

"And whatever you ask in prayer, you will receive, if you have faith." -Matthew 21:22

—

"Let no one deceive himself. If anyone among you thinks that he is wise in this age, let him become a fool that he may become wise. -1 Corinthians 13:8

—

"Speaking the truth in love, we are to grow up in every way into him who is the head, into Christ." -Ephesians 4:15

—-

"Therefore, as God's chosen people, holy and dearly loved, clothe yourselves with compassion, kindness, humility, gentleness and patience. Bear with each other and forgive one another if any of you has a grievance against someone. Forgive as the Lord forgave you. And over all these virtues put on love, which binds them all together in <u>perfect unity</u>. Let the peace of Christ rule in your hearts, since as members of one body you were called to peace. And be thankful. Let the message of Christ dwell among you richly as you teach and admonish one another with all wisdom through psalms, hymns, and songs from the Spirit, singing to God with gratitude in your hearts. And whatever you do, whether in word or deed, do it all in the name of the Lord Jesus, giving thanks to God the Father through him." -Colossians 3:12

—

Jesus answered, "I am the way and the truth and the life. No one comes to the Father except through me." - John 14:6

—

"For God so loved the world that he gave his one and only Son, that whoever believes in him shall not perish but have eternal life." -John 3:16

—

"Blessed are the pure in heart, for they shall see God."
-Matthew 5:8

—

God *gave* His son. To love is to give of ourselves, especially our time and love.

"GIVE and it will be given to you. A good measure, pressed down, shaken together and running over, will be poured into your lap. For with the measure you use, it will be measured to you." -Luke 6:38

—

"Now that you have purified yourselves by <u>obeying the truth</u> so that you have sincere love for each other, love one another deeply, from the heart. For you have been born again, not of perishable seed, but of imperishable, through the living and enduring word of God. For,

"All people are like grass,

and all their glory is like the flowers of the field;

the grass withers and the flowers fall,

but the word of the Lord endures forever."

And this is the word that was preached to you."

1 Peter 22

B: Resources

If you received this book at no cost, please consider making a donation to our ministry to help us expand our reach here: www.paypal.me/markfjohnston

On the web

Blog, articles, publications: TreasureLifeMedia.Com

Order this book: TreasureLifeMedia.Com/LastBreakup

Proceeds

Donate to our ministry to help us spread the Gospel: www.paypal.me/markfjohnston.

A portion of all proceeds of this book will go to the Christian Haitian charity Kolej Project operated by our good friends, Dan and Zoe. https://kolejproject.org

Services

We can help you write your testimony book. Please contact us for details.

Social Media and Contacts

Facebook: www.facebook.com/markjohnstonwriter

Instagram: @markjohnstonwriter

Twitter: @markjwriter

LinkedIn: LinkedIn.com/in/markfjohnston

Email: treasurelifemedia@gmail.com

The *Last* Breakup

C: Copyright Notices

Light and Darkness

Now there was a Pharisee, a man named Nicodemus who was a member of the Jewish ruling council. He came to Jesus at night and said, "Rabbi, we know that you are a teacher who has come from God. For no one could perform the signs you are doing if God were not with him."

Jesus replied, "Very truly I tell you, no one can see the kingdom of God unless they are born again.

"How can someone be born when they are old?" Nicodemus asked. "Surely they cannot enter a second time into their mother's womb to be born!"

Jesus answered, "Very truly I tell you, no one can enter the kingdom of God unless they are born of water and the Spirit. Flesh gives birth to flesh, but the Spirit gives birth to spirit.

For God so loved the world that he gave his one and only Son, that whoever believes in him shall not perish but have eternal life. For God did not send his Son into the world to condemn the world, but to save the world through him… This is the verdict: Light has come into the world, but people loved darkness instead of light because their deeds were evil. Everyone who does evil hates the light, and will not come into the light for fear that their deeds will be exposed. But whoever lives by the truth comes into the light, so that it may be seen plainly that what they have done has been done in the sight of God….

The one who comes from heaven is above all. He testifies to what he has seen and heard, but no one accepts his testimony. Whoever has accepted it has certified that God is truthful. For the one whom God has sent speaks the words of God, for God gives the Spirit without limit. The Father loves the Son and has placed everything in his hands. Whoever believes in the Son has eternal life, but whoever rejects the Son will not see life, for God's wrath remains on them." (John 3:1-36 NIV)

Thank you for reading our testimony.

We hope it has blessed you greatly.

Please consider sharing it with someone

who might benefit from it also. <3

Made in the
USA
Columbia, SC